FIVE
PENNIES

The General Store. Inside was everything in the world, including licorice.
Illustration by Brent Rambie.

FIVE PENNIES

A Prairie Boy's Story

IRENE MORCK

FIFTH
HOUSE
PUBLISHERS

Cover image (left to right): Arnfield, Archie, and Esther Morck in front of their log house, Dickson, Alberta, 1920.

Back cover and frontispiece illustrations by Brent Rambie. Log house illustration by Brent Rambie based on original artwork by Thora Kemtrup.

Cover and interior design by Brian Smith / Articulate Eye Design, Saskatoon, Saskatchewan.

The publisher gratefully acknowledges the support of The Canada Council for the Arts and the Department of Canadian Heritage.

THE CANADA COUNCIL | LE CONSEIL DES ARTS
FOR THE ARTS | DU CANADA
SINCE 1957 | DEPUIS 1957

We acknowledge the financial support of the Government of Canada through the Book Publishing Industry Development Program for our publishing activities.

First published in the United States in 1999.

Printed in Canada.

99 00 01 02 03 / 5 4 3 2 1

CANADIAN CATALOGUING IN PUBLICATION DATA

Morck, Irene.

 Five pennies

ISBN 1-894004-32-9

1. Morck, Archie. 1910-1976. 2. Dickson Region (Alta.)—Biography. 3. Frontier and pioneer life—Alberta—Dickson Region 4. Danish Canadians—Alberta—Dickson Region. 5. Dickson Region (Alta.)—History I. Title

FC3699.D52Z49 1999   971.2'3302'092   C99-910715-1   F1079.5.D49M67 1999

Fifth House Ltd.
#9 - 6125 11 St. SE
Calgary, AB, Canada
T2H 2L6

Published in the U.S. by Fitzhenry & Whiteside
121 Harvard Ave.
Suite 2
Allston, Massachusetts
02134

DEDICATION

For my wonderful dad, who dreamed that the stories he lived would become a book, for my aunts Thora and Esther, who helped tremendously, and for my family, who never quit believing that a dream can come true.

Now Ruthie can say, "I told you so."

CONTENTS

Acknowledgements

Thank you to Brian Smith for the outstanding cover, to Sheila Bean for great editing, to Charlene Dobmeier for encouragement and acceptance, to Brent Rambie for beautiful artwork, and to everyone else who had a part in creating this book.

CRASH LANDING

I must have been about five years old when I saw my first falling cow.

There in the dark, musty old barn, late in 1915, maybe early 1916, Mama and Papa perched on their three-legged milk stools, squirting warm, foaming milk into cold metal pails. My little brother, Arnfeld, huddled against me in the corner of the old barn.

I daydreamed, a sleepy and happy boy, cosy, sheltered from the howling Saskatchewan prairie winter wind, vaguely aware of the familiar, almost pleasant smell of fresh, steaming cow manure.

My eyes followed a few little puffs of dust and straw as they sifted gently downwards from the layer of dirt and straw covering the ancient scrap-board roof of our ramshackle barn. My parents had piled that dirt and straw on top of the rickety roof to help keep out the wind and weather.

Suddenly, overhead, we all heard it . . . Something walking?

"What the . . . ?" yelled Papa, jumping to his feet.

CRASH! The roof gave way. Down tumbled a sprawling cow, broken boards, straw, and dirt, right on top of Martha, the young cow that Papa had been milking.

Wood bounced off Papa's shoulder. Jumping out of the way, Mama tripped in the gutter, spilling her milk pail. The fallen unknown cow moaned, her skinny sides heaving, her legs flailing. Without even trying to get up, she snitched some straw, chewing frantically as though she hadn't eaten for weeks.

Pinned underneath the fallen cow, our own cow Martha bellowed, squirming in the greasy manure, fighting the wooden stanchion holding her head.

Our other cattle wrestled against their stanchions and joined in the desperate bawling. The horses snorted and screamed, yanking back on their halter ropes. Through the gaping roof, prairie winter cut into every corner of the barn, swirling straw, dust, and snow into our faces.

All the frantic eyes, shining in the flicker of the lantern, sent shivers through me as I watched Papa struggle to help the two animals to their feet.

Then Papa gritted his teeth, grabbed the lantern from its hook, and ran into the freezing night with Mama, Arnfeld, and me following close behind.

In the flickering light of the lantern we found that the snow had drifted up the back of the barn, right to the roof, forming a solid, white ramp. And on that snowdrift ramp was a set of hoofprints all the way to the top.

"She must have smelled the straw sticking out of the snow on the roof and climbed up to try to eat it," said Mama. "Poor cow."

"Those blasted neighbours!" Papa muttered. "If they'd feed their animals, they wouldn't be wandering around here. Could have killed us."

Trembling, I leaned against Mama. Immediately she wrapped an arm around me. She knew right away that I was trembling more from fear than from cold. "Don't worry, Archie," she said. "The cows aren't hurt, and all four of us are fine. Don't worry."

Papa hollered, "We can't stand out here babbling all night in this wind and forty below. We've got to patch up that hole."

It seemed to take forever to fix the roof well enough to keep the animals sheltered for the night. Up the snowdrift ramp we trudged, carrying load after load of scrap boards. With numb hands we tied the scraps of wood together with old, rusty wire, bracing ourselves against the cutting wind and swirling snow.

When we finally finished patching the roof, we reluctantly carried up straw to stuff between the cracks to keep out the wind. Papa said, "We still have to dig away the bottom of the snowdrift. Otherwise it'll just happen again." So my weary parents tried to shovel out the base of the rock-hard drift, but every shovelful of snow was replaced in a few minutes by more snow, courtesy of the determined wind.

The next morning we checked carefully for stray cows before we entered the barn. Arnfeld and I huddled together as Mama and Papa sat on their milk stools, their backs tense, their heads cocked to listen above the swoosh, swoosh of milk into the pails, listening for noises on the roof.

It was several days later, when we had begun to relax, that it happened again. And again. Once a cow even landed right on the head of a horse, knocking it unconscious.

Each time, after tending to a fallen cow and to any other creature in the path of her descent, we'd be patching that roof again.

When spring finally came, we moved to a new farm with a barn that had a roof made of real lumber—with no covering of straw to entice hungry cattle. And that's why I was about five years old when I saw my *last* falling cow, too.

SLOP PAILS AND A POCKET WATCH

Very early memories hang in patches, difficult to match, frayed and ragged around the edges. I remember nothing of the place in Manitoba where I was born, and other than the falling cows, most of my memories of Saskatchewan are faded, nearly gone. One, however, remains indelible.

In the autumn, when I had just turned six years old, I helped one of Papa's friends by picking up his hundreds and hundreds of potatoes and dropping them into pails as the man dug loose each potato hill. It involved a lot of bending and lifting, but I felt proud to be able to do it.

A few days later the man arrived at our house. "I've brought Archie a present," he said, handing me a small package.

Excited, I opened it, but nothing could have prepared me for what I saw. A Pocket Ben watch! I could not believe it. Those watches cost a whole dollar, a full day's wage for a grown man.

Papa protested. "You can't give a watch like that to a boy."

"I want him to have it," the man said. "Archie did a great job helping me with the potatoes."

"You'll have to take it back. He's too young, much too young to have a watch," Papa said. "He won't take care of it."

Mama glanced sideways at Papa, then spoke quietly, but oh, so firmly. "I can sew a strong little pocket inside his pants and tie the watch to it with a sturdy piece of string."

That night Mama taught me how to tell time. For the next few days I did my chores eagerly, timing everything. I timed how long it took me to peel potatoes and carrots. I timed how long it took to carry the wood. I timed how long it took to do the dishes.

Of course we didn't have any running water or any plumbing in those days, so all kitchen waste was dumped into slop pails. It took me six and a half minutes to carry the little pail from the house to the barn to feed the slop to the pigs.

One morning when Mama carried out the big slop pail, she returned swinging the empty bucket in one hand, waving a table fork in the other. "Archie, see what I found when I dumped the slop into the pig trough."

She laughed. "Potato peelings, old dishwater, coffee grounds, leftover food. Yes, that's all slop. But not cutlery." Her eyes twinkled. "Pigs can't use forks. Their manners aren't that good."

Then her voice took on a more serious tone. "I wonder who let that fork go into the slop pail. Could it be somebody is too busy looking at his new watch to check the dirty dishwater before he empties it into the pail?" That's all she said, but I never again forgot to run my hands carefully through the water before pouring it into the slop pail.

A few days later, climbing down the steep wooden stairs to the main floor of our house, I stumbled at the top. Down I slid on my stomach, bumping painfully along headfirst all the way down each step, gaining speed, unable to stop.

At the foot of the stairs was the huge slop pail waiting to be taken out to the pigs. Of course I landed right in it, submerging my right arm, my shoulders, and my whole head and face.

Without even moving my right arm from the overturned pail, I used my clean left hand to yank the watch from my sodden pocket. Aching all over, shaking stinky scraps out of my hair, blinking through my sloppy eyelashes, I peered at my watch. It was still running.

THE GOPHER MAN

I knew almost no English before I started school. True, I'd been born in Canada, but my two Danish-immigrant parents had settled in a Danish farming community in Saskatchewan, so Danish was all we heard at first.

Within a few months of grade one, English had taken over as my language, even my thinking.

At first Papa tried to legislate. "Archie, you can speak all the English you want away from home, but at our place you must use Danish—only Danish."

That soon became a dead law. Gradually even my father began to converse in English with Danish people who came to visit in our home, people who had been learning English from their school-age children, too.

I often heard my father and other Danish immigrant men, speaking in English, discussing the "gopher man." I knew the gopher as a little rodent that burrowed underground, a nuisance to farmers. But who was this "gopher man"? The way they talked, he was far more than a nuisance. They despised him.

I listened as they stated bitterly, "The gopher man cheated us." Many times they talked in contradictory terms. "The gopher man can't do anything." And yet, "The gopher man is too powerful."

They discussed what he should do. "The gopher man should step in." (Step in what?) "The gopher man should spend more money." Yet often they complained, "The gopher man is broke."

He seemed powerful and yet useless, rich and yet bankrupt, and always wicked. Who was this gopher man? It baffled me.

Then one day when I was in grade two, eavesdropping on the older kids' history lesson, I heard our teacher with his British accent asking the students something about the federal and provincial governments. To my amazement a grade five boy, who still had a Danish accent, answered, "The Saskatchewan gopher man is responsible."

The teacher said, "It's pronounced gov-ern-ment!" Yes! Now, at last, I knew who the "gopher man" was. My immigrant father and his friends, with their heavy accents, had put their own twist on the word "government." And all they said was true. The gopher man did seem rich, yet broke, powerless, yet too powerful.

HEADING WEST

In early November 1917, when I was seven years old, I helped Papa build a wooden crate for Mama's beautiful, chrome-decorated wood cookstove. The stove, along with our family's other essential things, was shipped west on a freight train for six hundred miles.

Papa, Mama, my four-year-old brother Arnfeld, my baby sister Esther, and I followed on a passenger train.

We were moving to the Danish community of Dickson in the central Alberta woodlands, leaving all of our friends, a beautiful two-storey house, and a well-developed, rented farm on the Saskatchewan prairies.

We were going to be pioneers, taking over a quarter-section, mostly uncleared, from a homesteader who had given up. We'd own our own land! And we'd get to live in a real log house—only two rooms, Papa had said, but at least it would be ours. Arnfeld and I were particularly excited about the log house.

For some reason Mama didn't share our sense of adventure. In fact, during the last few days, Mama had seemed quiet and far away.

It sure didn't cheer her up when all of her friends cried and cried as they hugged us and said goodbye.

As we climbed into the train car, Arnfeld gasped, "Ah, pretty." I was supposed to be a tough guy, already seven years old, but I had to agree. The train car was pretty. Shimmering mirrors all along the walls reflected image after image, countless images, of smooth, carved oak furnishings and intricately woven reed seats.

It didn't take many hours, though, for my little brother and me to decide that the fancy seats were uncomfortable. "Archie and Arnfeld, behave," commanded our father every time we squirmed too much.

The steam train huffed and puffed its way slowly along the prairies. Mama stared out the window. I was wishing she'd joke with us or tell us stories.

When darkness came, Arnfeld and I watched uniformed conductors light the gas lamps, moving effortlessly through the train, swaying with its clickety-clack through miles of night. Our baby sister, Esther, seemed to like the rhythm, for she slept peacefully in Mama's arms, undisturbed by the shrill train whistle piercing the prairie silence. I leaned against Arnfeld and nodded off to sleep.

Morning arrived. Arnfeld and I awoke, stiff from sitting, but still excited. All that next day the train chugged west over endless, lonely prairie. Mile after mile of sagebrush, wheat stubble, and dry, brown grass poked through the dirty snow and wind-brushed soil. And all day long, Mama attended to us without her usual smiles.

Night again. Once more we slept to the rhythm of wheels and the cry of a train whistle.

The second morning we awoke to a scene of red brick buildings, more buildings than I had ever dreamed existed.

"That's Calgary," Papa told us. We stared, wordless. Our mother hardly said anything, not even when the train pulled into the station.

In Calgary we boarded another train, headed north towards Innisfail at the edge of Alberta's woodland area. Little could I have imagined that we would not return to Calgary for another fourteen years, even though this city was less than one hundred miles away from our new homestead.

At Innisfail a man named Henry Larsen met us in an open Ford car. He'd be taking us west to Dickson. Papa already knew Mr. Larsen, and other people in Dickson, too, from his visit two months ago when he had found us our farm.

When Papa told us that we were about to ride in one of the few cars of the Dickson community, we felt privileged.

Shivering, we crowded into Mr. Larsen's car and headed west, the wind blowing through our hair. The dirt trail wound over heavily wooded hills. "I didn't know there were so many trees in the whole world," I said.

Mr. Larsen smiled. "No? Not if you've always lived on the prairies."

"We had some little poplars and willows on the prairies. In the coulees," I said. "Papa always cut the biggest poplar he could find for a Christmas tree. Sometimes he'd even find one as tall as me. And Mama makes better Christmas tree decorations than anybody else." I expected Mama to say something funny, but she just shook her head.

Mr. Larsen smiled and pointed. "Those tall, bare trees, they're poplars. Same as yours on the prairie, just a lot bigger. And the bare bushes are willows. Those other trees, those big green ones, they're spruce. They keep their nice, green needles all winter long. You'll have real Christmas trees around here."

Arnfeld and I grinned. Mama said that would be very nice.

About a mile out of Innisfail the rutty trail became steep, twisting up and down sand hills. Mama clasped Esther to her chest. "Boys, hang on tight or you'll fall out."

Mr. Larsen slowed the car. "Sorry, Mrs. Morck. I forget. You're used to flat, straight roads."

She tried to smile. "I guess everything's going to be different," she said.

We came to a steep riverbank. The car seemed to point straight down. Mama's face showed her terror. "Boys, please hold on tight!"

We reached the bridge and river. I'd seen only little creeks on the prairies. This was a real river. The car wheels bumped along, farther and farther, over the bridge's loose, uneven planks. Would these planks hold the weight of the car and all of us? I knew Mama was wondering, too.

"Sure is a big river," I ventured when we were only about halfway across.

"It's called the Red Deer River," said Mr. Larsen. "This river runs right through a corner of your farm, so you'll be able to play on its banks." Arnfeld and I looked at each other, our eyes wide.

Finally reaching the other side of the bridge, the car crawled, roaring, up the sharp incline. West of the river the land levelled off.

We were back in the bushes and trees again. Once in a while we saw a small house and tiny patches of land that had been cleared into fields.

While we boys admired trees, Papa and Mr. Larsen talked. "I've made arrangements," said Mr. Larsen. "All of you can stay a few days with Pastor and Mrs. Andersen in their parsonage in Dickson. That way, Mr. Morck, you can get things ready at your new farm before you move your whole family."

Arnfeld and I looked at each other, our eyes glowing. The adventure was about to begin. If only Mama would understand and appreciate how lucky we were to be living on a pioneer homestead, in a log house.

Dickson, 1917

When we finally reached Dickson we were surprised at how small it was. Dickson in 1917 was hardly anything: a one-room school, a church, four houses, three barns, and one general store.

That afternoon in Dickson, Mama and baby Esther had a rest at Pastor and Mrs. Andersen's place while Papa walked across the road, with his two little shadows trotting behind, to the big white building with a sign proclaiming "CARL CHRISTIANSEN, GENERAL STORE."

A bell tinkled as we entered.

Inside was everything in the world, including licorice.

The owner of this store (and of the licorice) was Carl Christiansen, a sturdy, red-haired man. We watched him give out mail to a few people, smiling and chatting to each one. When Carl Christiansen noticed us standing there, he came from his post office cubicle to shake hands enthusiastically with Papa. "Good to see you again, Mr. Morck. We are so glad you decided to come and live in Dickson."

The other people standing around spoke warmly to Papa while I stared at the licorice.

Carl Christiansen turned his wonderful smile towards us boys. "And who are you two?"

"I'm Archie Morck. We just came from Saskatchewan."

"I'm Arnfeld Morck. I'm four years old."

"Well, I'm Uncle Carl. Good to see some more young boys moving in here. Maybe we can get a ball team going," he said with a cheerful, booming voice. Then, to my astonishment, he slipped a licorice stick into the front pocket of my pants and did the same to Arnfeld. We didn't even have to share!

"Come on upstairs," he said. "My wife probably has the coffee pot on. Maybe we'll find some fresh-baked cookies for you boys. And you can meet my children."

By the time we tore ourselves away from Carl Christiansen's place, it was dark and suppertime at the Andersens'.

The next morning Papa bought an old wagon, a team of horses, and a cow from some people in the area. Then it was time to get things settled at our new homestead. Another two neighbours were in the wagon, ready to help. I was a bit annoyed when Papa said that I'd just be in the way if I came along.

So I watched Papa and the other men load our things from back home, including Mama's fancy stove, of course, to take them out to the farm. They tied our new cow to the back of the wagon and headed off, with Arnfeld and me waving goodbye.

That afternoon, Arnfeld and I explored the tiny settlement of Dickson while Mama stayed with Mrs. Andersen and looked after our baby sister.

Arnfeld and I decided to investigate the church last because we had never been in a church before and weren't sure if we should be going inside.

Dickson had one intersection. Behind the parsonage, which was on the northwest corner of the intersection, we saw a barn. Inside we patted Pastor Andersen's milk cows and his team of horses.

On the northeast corner of the intersection stood Carl Christiansen's store. Of course we went in to say good morning to our new friend, "Uncle Carl." This time he didn't give us any licorice, but was very friendly. So were all of the customers. With a wistful glance at the licorice, we left the store to continue our tour.

East of the store stood the schoolhouse. We could hear the sounds of school in session. What kind of friends would I meet there next week? Would there be bullies? When they found out that my middle name was Nicholaj, would they tease me with "Nicholaj-Pickle-Eye," as the kids in Saskatchewan had done, running after me until I cried? What would the teacher be like?

Arnfeld and I sneaked inside the school barn and patted the horses.

Across the street, to the south, was the church and an open area. East of that were three houses, one of them painted green. Mr. Pedersen, who lived there, invited us in for a cookie and told us that he was called "Green House Pedersen" to distinguish him from the many other Pedersens in the district.

"Green House Pedersen" told us that in one of the other two houses there also lived a Mr. Pedersen. That one spent his winters trapping muskrats and was called, of course, "Muskrat Pedersen."

Finally we stood in front of the beautiful white church. "Look how high the tower is," I said in awe. "And the cross on top. And look at the huge bell."

"Do you think we could go inside?" asked my little brother. "I've never been in a church."

"Me neither." In fact we'd never even seen a church. We'd been to Sunday services near Redvers every month or so, but these services had been conducted by visiting pastors, held in farmhouses or outside in farmyards in good weather.

Now here we were, about to enter a real church.

We paused a few minutes to swing on the long, well-worn wooden hitching rail, then summoned enough courage to march up the steps of the church. Pushing the heavy wooden door gently, we peeked in.

"Ah." Our whispers echoed in the empty building. Not daring to step inside, we gazed at a painting set in an intricately carved frame. To our amazement, it was just like one of the coloured pictures in Mama's Bible: Mary was kneeling in front of Jesus by the open tomb on Easter Sunday.

We stared at the rows of shiny wooden benches, at the organ with its back turned towards us, and at the altar with its tall, white, unlit candles. We stared and stared but never dared to step inside. With a click we closed the door and walked down the steps.

The clearing east of the church had several mounds of dirt, all of them nicely raked over, like flowerbeds that have been prepared for winter. In front of some of the smooth "beds" were words carved into large, shiny pieces of rock. Each rock showed a name, some numbers, and some Danish words.

Reading those words proved difficult. Although Arnfeld and I spoke much more Danish than English, my year of schooling in Saskatchewan had all been in English. Still, Mama had taught me to read a little Danish. "It says something about 'with Jesus,'" I told my brother.

We moved on to a very small mound of dirt. Again I struggled, trying to read the Danish words on the rock.

"This one has something about a little lamb," I said, shaking my head, totally puzzled.

THE ESSENTIALS

At last came the afternoon when Papa declared that he had moved all of the essential things to our new farm. We could move into our new home!

The wagon was crammed with our family and with more last-minute groceries from Carl Christiansen's general store. Calling out to the Andersens, "Thanks" and "See you in church on Sunday," we rumbled off. I could hardly wait to see the farm. I just wished Mama would look a bit more enthusiastic. Why wasn't she excited to get a first look at our very own real log cabin?

It was a crisp, sunny November afternoon. Very little snow covered the ground. The wagon bumped and swayed over the four-mile trail that wound among bushes, trees, and frozen sloughs. What a lot of unused land! Mama looked even more depressed.

The wagon bumped across swamps on log trails called corduroy roads. Someone had laid these logs down. I wondered who. The logs were worn and frozen in place so I knew Papa hadn't put them there. There seemed to be no other people living here. We'd been in the wagon more than an hour without seeing anyone.

We turned a corner, and there, in a clearing, stood a log house. "That's our place," said Papa.

I leaped out of the wagon, nearly dancing with excitement. "A real log cabin! Real logs! Look at the corners! How did they get the logs together at the corners? And what's the stuff between the logs?"

"It's plaster," Papa answered. "They mix sand with lime to make it."

"What's the black stuff on the roof?" asked Arnfeld.

"Tar paper," said Papa. "To keep out rain or snow."

"How come we didn't have tar paper on our other house?"

"Because it had shingles."

The cabin looked so rustic and intriguing from the outside. But when we opened the door, our excitement vanished. We stared into the dark interior, all of us quiet.

Dirty, water-stained, faded paper was tacked over the walls. Dusty shreds of torn paper hung down, exposing dingy, rough logs underneath.

There were only two small rooms. I'd known that before, but somehow it had never hit me how crowded only two rooms might be for a family of five.

One room was a kitchen, with our table, chairs, and all of the pantry things. The other small room obviously was to be a combined sitting-room/bedroom, stuffed with our couch and chair, my parents' double bed, the baby crib, and a little bed for my brother and me.

The partition, between the two rooms, and the ceiling itself were both just networks of crudely nailed-together spruce saplings with filthy, sagging paper tacked here and there. There was no door to close between the two rooms, simply a gaping door frame of more spruce saplings.

I turned to Mama to see her reaction. She looked terribly discouraged. She walked over to her beloved kitchen stove, touched it like a dear old friend, then quietly began unpacking.

A few minutes later, Mama stopped and went outside for wood so she could start a fire in her stove. That stove was from the beautiful two-storey farmhouse on the prairies. A world away.

When Papa went out to feed the animals and milk the cow, Mama stoked the fire, then searched for the pots and pans.

The short November daylight was fading so I helped Mama unpack our kerosene lamps. Some of the glass chimneys had broken during the move. "Good thing we bought a couple of new chimneys from Carl Christiansen," Mama said.

"Twelve cents each," chirped Arnfeld, who had just learned his numbers.

"Hand me the kerosene can, Archie," Mama said. She poured the kerosene through the funnel into the glass belly of the lamp, trimmed the cotton wick with her scissors, and added a new glass chimney.

The soft glow made the cabin seem a bit more cosy. I stared at my reflection in the glass chimney, then looked right through to Mama's sad face, watching as she filled the heavy, tin-framed kerosene lantern.

"Here, Archie," she said, "take this outside to Papa. He'll hardly be able to see to milk the cow. It sure gets dark fast these days."

By the time I returned to the house, Mama was mixing dough for baking-powder biscuits. She handed me the frying pan. "Would you like to fry some bacon and eggs, Archie?"

Soon the kitchen was filled with the smell of sizzling bacon, and I began to feel more cheerful.

When Papa came in with the fresh milk, we sat down to supper—Mama and Papa on our two chairs, Arnfeld and I on a trunk, and our baby sister, Esther, in her high chair. I tried to avoid looking into the scary shadows, lurking all around those ugly walls. We ate, talking very little.

As the last biscuit and the last slice of bacon disappeared from our plates, someone knocked on the door. Who could that be?

We sat silent as Papa got up to open the door. A short, stocky man stood there, carrying a lantern, lighting our house brighter as he entered.

In a booming voice, he introduced himself. "I'm your neighbour, Soren Peder Lonneberg. But everybody just calls me S.P."

He handed Mama something wrapped in a dishtowel and said, "My wife sent this loaf of bread, fresh out of the oven. She'll be over to meet you first thing in the morning—she and a few of our many children. We live just half a mile away."

Then at last a smile brightened Mama's tired face. She cradled the loaf of bread in one arm while she dug around in the boxes of groceries to find the new tin of strawberry jam.

Slicing off a thick piece of Mrs. Lonneberg's warm, fragrant bread, Mama spread a layer of our jam over it, lifted the slice of bread high, grinned, and said, "Dessert!"

Neighbourly Advice

That first night, Mr. Lonneberg seemed to know how much we needed him there, and he stayed for almost two hours.

"Looks like you folks are getting settled in fine," said Mr. Lonneberg, glancing around the room. "My wife and I had a lot more to learn when we moved here. Imagine, we came straight from the big city of Chicago. Straight from a big city to be farmers on a pioneer homestead. We knew absolutely nothing about animals or crops or farm equipment or anything."

He laughed. "I was a carpenter. At least, Chris Morck, you've farmed before. That will be a lot of help. But I'll bet you'll find things are pretty backwards here compared to what you're used to." He was looking at Mama. "Including a two-room log house."

Mama nodded, but at least she was smiling now. Mr. Lonneberg pointed to Mama's stove and said, "That's a fine-looking cookstove."

Mama said, "We bought it almost a year ago in Saskatchewan. On Arnfeld's third birthday, actually."

Arnfeld tugged at Mr. Lonneberg's sleeve. "And I got to be the first to sit on the warming oven. Because it was my birthday."

Papa said, "Yeah, you could say that stove is Mama's pride and joy. Anyway, it does its job of cooking food and heating the kitchen."

Mr. Lonneberg said, "Talking about heating, do you know anything about the Little Wonder air-tight heater there?" He gestured to the other room.

"Not really," said Papa. "Never had a heater like that in Saskatchewan. Why?"

"We all use them around here. They're about the cheapest heaters you can get and they put out the most heat. Maybe that's why they're called 'Little Wonder.' But be careful. They're dangerous. They get hotter than you know what, and they've been the cause of many a house burning down. So watch real careful and don't stuff it too full of wood."

Mr. Lonneberg took a big sip of coffee. "You'll burn about twenty-five cords of wood a year to keep your cookstove and your Little Wonder going."

"What's a cord?" asked Papa. "On the prairies we always burn coal. Wood is too precious to be burned."

"When you clear your land here, you'll be setting fire to sky-high piles of trees, trying to get rid of them." Mr. Lonneberg smiled. "Anyway, a cord is an amount of wood that measures about as tall as little Archie here, about as wide as Archie if he were lying down, and about as long as two of him stretched out. So twenty-five cords is a lot of wood."

"Sounds like a lot of chopping," said Papa.

"Well, you have two fine boys here to help chop wood in the years to come."

"Sure. Why do you think I had my sons?" said Papa. The two men laughed.

"As soon as the snow is deep enough," said Mr. Lonneberg, "each farmer starts chopping trees and hauling them home. Most years the snow is already a foot deep by now. But I guess it'll come soon enough. In February we all help each other saw trees into blocks. Then each family splits their own firewood. I bet Archie is old enough to start splitting wood this winter."

He winked at me. "But you're a bit young to help build a barn." He looked at Papa. "Chris, you'll be needing a barn. If you chop down some good-sized poplar trees this week, all us neighbours will come next week and put up your barn."

Mama said, "We'd be grateful for that."

"Oh, we have to help each other around here." He smiled warmly at her then turned back to Papa.

Mr. Lonneberg kept talking. "We'll probably all be over next Thursday or so to build your barn. Maybe in a few years, when you're well-established, I can help you build a barn out of real lumber, but for now we'll start you out real simple with a nice log barn."

I wondered if Mama and Papa were going to tell Mr. Lonneberg that on the farm in Saskatchewan, we'd had a beautiful big barn made of solid lumber. But they didn't say anything. Maybe the lumber for that barn had come from Alberta.

Mr. Lonneberg continued. "There's a sawmill at Raven, just a few miles away. You'll need boards for some things, like for building granaries. Whenever you need lumber, you just load up a wagonful of logs that you've cut, haul them to the sawmill, and they'll saw them into boards. They'll keep part of the lumber for payment. Hardly anybody around here can pay them cash. You'll be lucky, like all of us, if you have enough cash in the years to come to buy nails."

"Well, I guess we have to walk before we can run," said Papa.

"That's the idea," said Mr. Lonneberg. "When we build your barn, we'll fill the cracks between the logs with wood splinters and then plaster the whole thing over with fresh cow manure."

"Cow manure?"

Mr. Lonneberg grinned. "Sure. Cow manure spreads real easy using a trowel. After we trowel it in, the manure dries or freezes, and stays in place a long time. In fact, I'd say cow manure is just as good as mortar. Besides, it's real plentiful and it's free."

Mr. Lonneberg kept the biggest surprise for the last. When he was getting ready to leave, he said, "Oh, by the way, Chris, make sure you cut some small poplar saplings for the roof. We'll cover the sapling roof with straw, and then guess what we'll put over the top of your new barn roof—a nice, thick layer of cow manure!"

Our eyes widened when we realized that he wasn't joking. "Cow manure really is just as good as mortar for sealing. It will dry and freeze and bind with the straw to make a good roof."

He laughed. "Only one drawback, I'd say. In a wet summer, when the rain pours down for days, there will be some water with a suspicious odour and a brown colour dripping down on your neck and on your back as you milk the cows. But maybe it's good for your skin, eh? Fertilizer, you know."

Both Mama and Papa looked paler than usual in the light of the coal oil lantern. "I guess we have to crawl before we can walk," Papa said, trying to smile.

"Yeah," said Mama, "We'd better go out there tonight and tell our new cows to get busy. Sounds as if they have quite a bit of roofing material to produce by next week."

CHURCH IN DICKSON

On our first Sunday in Alberta, we hooked up our new horses and wagon to head to Dickson for church. I was really looking forward to experiencing an actual church service, and it would be fun to meet some of my future school chums.

From the moment we arrived at the church, we felt surrounded with welcome. We didn't have much time to talk to anyone, though, because the huge bell was calling us inside for the worship service.

Into the church we went and sat on shiny wooden pews. In front of the altar Pastor Andersen stood all dressed up in a black gown and a stiff, white collar.

The choir stood to sing. Their director, Fred Pedersen, waved a violin bow up and down and around, his head rocking, one foot beating out the time, obviously loving what he was doing.

A young man faced the congregation at the organ, playing fantastic music, the tan-coloured cloth at the back of the organ breathing in and out, in and out.

The whole congregation—old people and young—sang hymns, many of which we'd sung at Sunday "church" picnics on various farms in Saskatchewan. It felt good to join in with these new people, to be part of their enthusiasm. I looked at Mama. She seemed so much happier than she had a few days ago.

The pastor prayed and preached. Everything was in Danish, some of the language too difficult for me to understand. But that didn't matter.

It all seemed so grand. Everything.

As soon as the church service finished, a little old lady came up to me, her face radiant against her conservative, dark clothes. "You must be Archie Morck. I'm Mrs. Laursen, and I've heard that you're seven years old."

I nodded.

"Good. Then you'll be in my Sunday School class. I teach all the seven-year-olds. After church there's always an hour of Sunday school for the children while the adults visit."

Mrs. Laursen put her arm around me, introduced me to the eight other children in her class, then led us to the front of the church at the left side.

Some children of our class sat on the floor, some sat on the front pew. One of the boys slid along the pew, motioning for me to sit beside him. I smiled. Maybe he could be my friend in school.

To my surprise, Mrs. Laursen knelt down on the floor in front of us. The other children seemed to think nothing of this old woman kneeling on the floor, so I realized this was her habit. It made sense. We could all pay attention, sitting there around her.

The Sunday School had no shortage of pupils—most pioneers followed literally the Bible verse, "Be fruitful and multiply." The air was alive with the murmur of classes all over the church, grouped according to age.

There were no partitions or Sunday School rooms. Each teacher simply gathered his or her pupils in a certain area, on the church pews. I waved at Arnfeld, and he grinned at me from his class.

Within a few minutes I was spellbound by Mrs. Laursen's Bible stories. There were no lesson books or special materials, but Mrs. Laursen brought the Biblical characters to life as though she personally knew each one of them.

I hoped my teacher at school could be as kind and interesting, but thought there wasn't much chance of that. Still, at least these kids in my Sunday School were going to be in my regular school class and they seemed very friendly.

The kids in my Saskatchewan school had often teased me so badly that I'd cry and then they'd tease me more. Now I actually found myself looking forward to going to school again. Maybe tomorrow Papa would bring me back to Dickson so I could start school.

I looked around the church at all the friendly faces and was glad that we had moved. Even Mama was smiling broadly as she visited with the new people.

~~

ALADDIN LAMP

When church was all over, and we were ready to go home to our new farm, the choir director, Fred Pedersen, stood talking by our wagon.

I admired the small, round bowler hat that perched on his soft, dark hair, and how his face glowed with kindness. "Make sure you folks—the whole family of you—come to choir practice at my place on Wednesday night," Fred Pedersen said.

"We can't sing," stated Papa. "I can't sing. Mama can't sing. Neither can Archie and Arnfeld. None of us can hold a tune."

"Doesn't matter," Fred Pedersen said. "Everybody comes to choir practice. Everybody. Some sing, some don't." Then he laughed, the most beautiful deep belly laugh I'd ever heard.

All around, people stopped their visiting and joined in with Fred Pedersen's laughter. It was a contagious kind of laugh; you just couldn't help joining in. Even I joined in laughing, and I wasn't sure why.

"We have a great time at choir practice," Fred Pedersen said. "And you'll get to see my ornery Aladdin lamp."

"Ornery?" I asked.

Fred Pedersen's eyes twinkled. "Archie, all Aladdin lamps act ornery! Come to choir practice and see."

I had never seen an Aladdin lamp. I knew they burned much brighter than our kerosene lamps and cost much more. But ornery? I could hardly wait until Wednesday night.

When we arrived at Fred Pedersen's home, the Aladdin lamp filled the room with its brilliant white light. Fred laughed. "See how it burns bright now. Wait until we really need it to read our music."

As more and more people arrived, the lamplight faded. The moment that the singing started, that Aladdin lamp faltered and almost died. The more powerfully we sang, the lower the lamp burned until we were truly singing in the dark.

"See this crazy lamp!" muttered Fred, shaking his head. "It

works well when we really don't need it. But as soon as we need it to read the music, then it won't work. It's just plain ornery."

We all laughed with him, and the lamp dimmed even more, the room becoming almost pitch dark, until I was positive that the lamp had actually gone out. But as soon as choir practice stopped and people sat down to visit, the lamp sprang to life.

When most of the people said goodnight and left, we watched the lamp burn even more brightly, like the sun. "Sure is an ornery lamp!" we agreed, shaking our heads.

Many, many years later, sitting in a science class, I learned about oxygen, complete combustion, and incomplete combustion.

Of course! That was it. Fred Pedersen's Aladdin lamp had been a victim of incomplete combustion. The kerosene burned under pressure in the mantle, so a tremendous amount of oxygen was needed to feed its inefficient combustion. Singing and laughing would have robbed the lamp of oxygen. But who could have dreamed of such scientific principles then? No, in those days, we all had to agree that Aladdin lamps were just plain ornery.

NEW KID AT SCHOOL

School posed a problem: Dickson was four miles away. Papa was busy chopping down trees for our barn and for enough firewood to last us through the coming winter.

Papa certainly couldn't take time to drive me with the team and wagon to Dickson every morning and then come back and get me every afternoon. Even when Papa had chopped down enough trees, built the barn, and hauled and chopped a winter's supply of firewood, he would be too busy with farm work. School buses didn't exist in those days, at least not in this area of central Alberta.

"Archie can walk to school," said Papa.

"He's only seven!" said Mama. "It would take him at least an hour and a half to walk four miles. He'll need a horse."

"A horse just to ride to school? Impossible!" Papa said. "There's no money. Not for a horse to just stand around in the school barn all day. If we get a new horse it has to be used all day for working the fields. Archie can walk four miles."

"Eight miles," said Mama. "There and back."

"We have no money for a horse just to ride to school."

"It will soon be the dead of winter," Mama said. "A seven-year-old can't walk eight miles in the winter."

Papa frowned. "What if he walked to school and stayed overnight with the Andersens or somebody else in Dickson? The next day after school he could walk home. How about that? He'd be home every other night."

"Four miles is still too much."

"Don't you want him to go to school?"

Finally Papa's plan was agreed on. I was to walk four miles a day, for that winter anyway, and stay in Dickson on the nights in between. "When winter's over," said Papa, "Archie can walk eight miles a day, because we'll need him at home every night to help on the farm."

At least Papa brought me in the wagon to school the first morning. By then I was really looking forward to going to school.

At our first Sunday church service and at the Wednesday night choir practice I'd had a chance to talk to quite a few boys my age. I was eager to see them again at school. Maybe here I'd have some good friends.

When we arrived, it was still early. A few children were playing in the school yard. Papa tied our horses to the hitching rail and took me into the schoolhouse.

The teacher, Mr. Chadsey, was starting a fire in the heater to warm the one-room school. Papa introduced us. As we spoke, puffs of breath moved between us in the chilly November air.

"If Archie needs a strapping, give it to him," said Papa. "Don't let him get away with anything."

"He looks like a nice, quiet boy," said Mr. Chadsey. "I'm sure we'll get along fine."

After Papa left, Mr. Chadsey showed me to my desk and handed me some books. "Now, Archie, you go outside and play until school starts. Set your lunch pail in the hallway by the others. At recess all the children bring their lunch pails in here by the heater. That way you won't have to eat frozen sandwiches."

I played for a few minutes with my new friends until Mr. Chadsey stood on the steps ringing a handbell and we all ran to form a line. Into the classroom we marched.

Standing, we said the Lord's Prayer. Mr. Chadsey read a Bible story and then we all sang "The Maple Leaf Forever."

After the shuffling of fifty children settling at their desks, Mr. Chadsey introduced me to the students, then began organizing the eight grades.

I listened to the scratching and screeching of slate pencils on slate boards, and looked down at my slate, made like all the others, of black slate stone in a wooden frame edged with cotton. But this slate was different. It had come with me all the way from Saskatchewan, so it was my old friend. And the five slender, grey slate pencils laid out on my desk—they were from Saskatchewan, too. It seemed fine for the slate and my slate pencils—and me—to be here in Alberta, with friendly classmates and a kind teacher.

PLEASING PAPA

Every day at school, we younger children would be left to do our own assignments when our teacher, Mr. Chadsey, was busy with the older pupils. That's how it was in a one-room school.

When I was supposed to be working on my own lessons, I had a hard time resisting the temptation to eavesdrop on those more advanced lessons. Especially tempting were the grades seven and eight history lessons. How could grade one arithmetic compete with stories of King Henry VIII divorcing or murdering his wives for having baby girls instead of baby boys?

How could a young kid concentrate on grade one grammar when the older students were discussing the "Poke," a mysterious man with authority over the kings and queens of Europe?

Astounded, I overheard the story of how the Poke made King Henry IV dress in rags and stand barefoot in the snow for days, pleading to be allowed to kneel at the Poke's feet to receive forgiveness for some deed. This Poke must have been the most powerful reprobate who ever ruled anywhere.

Eventually I realized that the word was "Pope," not "Poke," but for a child exposed to Lutheran doctrines only, the concept of divine authority was overwhelming.

The Pope might have ruled kings and queens, but in our home Papa ruled—with an iron hand.

Papa did not believe in sparing the rod nor spoiling the child. We were all expected to work hard at a very early age, and we were expected to do our work carefully, whether it be washing dishes, digging up the garden, or chopping wood.

"Any fool can break a handle," Papa would say. If we were digging or chopping and did break a handle of a pitchfork or of an axe, no excuse would be accepted. Because he made harness, Papa could always find plenty of leather scraps with which he inflicted instant and stinging punishment.

Terrified of Papa's harsh discipline, I told lie after lie, weaving elaborate networks of tales that usually trapped me anyway into more stinging encounters with pieces of leather. And if I cried, Papa would strap harder. I grew more afraid of the strappings and more tempted to lie about my wrongdoings.

There was a belief in those days that every white speck on a person's fingernails represented one lie that he or she had told. Probably the many knocks and bangs of farm work had put all my white spots there, but I became so self-conscious that I developed a habit of folding my fingers into a fist or keeping my hands tucked in my pockets.

I felt so guilty and wicked for lying, fighting with my siblings, being careless, and all of the other things that I kept doing wrong. Why, oh, why did I keep disappointing my parents? I wondered if maybe they wished they'd never had me.

So I tried even harder to please them, feeling thrilled and proud of anything I might do to make them glad they had me.

Soon after we moved to Dickson, Papa bought more cows, so there was plenty of milking to do. I tried milking the tamest cow and still ended up with the cow kicking me or tipping the milk pail. Mama would say, "Archie, keep trying."

Eventually I could milk a cow without much ado, but when I figured the cow was all milked out, Papa would always sit down and "strip" her, getting half as much milk again. "You didn't milk her, Archie," he'd say, scowling. "You just got her started."

Mama always told me that I was doing fine so I'd keep trying to empty those udders. Still it seemed as though Papa would always be able to get more milk from any cow, when I was certain that I had finished milking her.

Then one evening, shortly after my eighth birthday, Papa sat down to strip the cow I had been milking. Nonchalantly he pulled on her teats, expecting to get his usual jet of milk.

Nothing?

Papa bent over and pulled again. And again. I stood watching, my heart thumping. Still nothing. Not one drop more could he get.

"I guess you've learned to milk a cow," was all he said. But coming from my father it seemed like fabulous praise. I flexed my aching hands and felt on top of the world.

Bedbug Ballad

Bedbugs appeared the first summer, 1918, after we moved to our two-room log house. Even now, I start scratching when I think about them. Bedbugs were the plague of pioneers who lived in old log cabins.

Every evening, as soon as the sun set, bedbugs by the hundreds crept out from between the logs to hunt for blood. We could hear them all through the night, humming their sinister, low-pitched hunting song.

We fought the bugs all through the night as they bit and sucked our blood until their bellies were swollen bright red. By morning we'd be covered with red welts so itchy and painful we'd feel like tearing off our skin.

Until then, homesteading in central Alberta's woodlands had been a challenge, but at least each day's work was rewarded by a good night's sleep. When the bedbugs appeared, our lives became unbearable.

We waged full-scale battle against the invaders, executing every bedbug we found. Still itching from previous nights, we carried our kerosene lamps into the dark sitting-room/bedroom, revealing the hated things as they scurried along the rough walls and ceiling. We'd hold the lamp under the bugs and listen for the heat to make them pop.

Everywhere we sprinkled insect powders (sprays were unknown then). We set the legs of our beds in cans of kerosene, hoping to drown any creatures trying to climb up from the floor. Along the edges of each mattress we spread tracks of kerosene mixed with turpentine, forming a barrier around our bodies. But those bedbugs seemed to drop on us from the ceiling.

Nothing seemed to help.

Finally we decided on gas warfare. Someone had told us that the fumes from burning sulphur would kill bedbugs, so Papa drove the team of horses to town and brought back thirty pounds of powdered sulphur. All we had to do was figure out how to set it on fire without burning down our house.

Our neighbour, S.P. Lonneberg, solved the problem. "Maybe you could burn it in your tank heater," he said. Out we marched to the barnyard to look at the tank heater that kept ice off the animals' drinking water.

The tank heater was a heavy, cast-iron cylinder with a short stovepipe and a small door for putting in wood. Yes, it could do the trick. With much huffing and puffing, Arnfeld and I helped Papa and Mr. Lonneberg drag the tank heater to the house and set it in the middle of the kitchen.

"The air in the house will be poison to people, too," Mr. Lonneberg warned. "You should stay with us for a couple of days."

Papa snorted. "Nah, I can sleep in an empty granary here. I have to be around to be sure the fire's all right. Archie and Arnfeld are old enough to sleep in the granary, too. But if Mama and little Esther could stay with you, that would be good."

Mr. Lonneberg nodded. "And we have to move all your food out. I'll bring it in the wagon to our place."

Mama asked, "What about the silverware? They say sulphur will turn any silver black."

Papa scowled. "We can't worry about little things like that! Just wrap the silverware in linen or paper and pack it away in a drawer."

At last everything was ready. Mr. Lonneberg drove his wagon out of the yard with Mama, Esther, and the food.

Arnfeld and I helped Papa build a grand fire in the tank heater. Then, with a vengeance, we poured in all of the sulphur. Out we raced, slamming the door.

We peered in the window. Within seconds, thick, white smoke filled the house and reached us outside, tearing at our lungs and throats. Still we had to stay, choking and coughing, watching through the window to be sure the house was safe.

Suddenly an intense blue flame rose right out of the tank heater's short stovepipe. The fire roared. The blue flame leaped from the stovepipe, higher and higher, almost to the ceiling now.

Frantically Papa looked around. "That basin. Archie, get me that basin. If I run in and put it over the top of the stovepipe, it might control the flame."

I brought the basin, my stomach tight. "Papa, the air in there is poison."

"I'll hold my breath. We can't let the house burn down."

"No! Papa, please. No!"

He grabbed a long piece of rope. "I'll tie this around my waist.

You boys watch me through the window. If the gas knocks me out, you both pull on the rope and drag me outside."

Gulping, I nodded, and he disappeared into the thick smoke. Watch him? We couldn't even see him. How would we know if we should be pulling him out?

But then we saw the flame capped down and the outline of the basin through the smoke.

A violently coughing body hurtled out, slammed the door, and collapsed. We rushed over to Papa as he sprawled on the grass, coughing as though he would choke to death, his eyes red and wet. "Papa, what should we do?" I sobbed.

He couldn't answer, and just gestured for us to get away.

Within a few minutes his coughing eased. Then Papa stood up and seemed as healthy as ever.

Throughout the night the sulphur burned. It was hard to sleep when we were so excited. We kept getting up to check on the state of affairs in the house. Twinkling stars and a fingernail clipping of a moon added a touch of magic to the eerie blue flame and the white smoke that filled the darkness in our log house.

By morning the flame had died and the sulphur was gone. Choking, our eyes and throats burning, we ran in and opened the windows. The floor was crunchy with countless dead bodies. Even Papa couldn't stop smiling.

"I hope they suffered a lot," said my little brother, laughing, "just as much as they made us suffer."

We left the house open so the poison gas could escape, then went over to the Lonneberg farm with the good news.

Two days later we moved back into our house. When Mama unpacked the silverware she exclaimed, "Look! Black as coal! I should have taken it with me." But still Mama was smiling because the task of polishing silver seemed like nothing compared to our victory against the bugs. Not a live one anywhere! What joy to be able to sleep without being bitten.

Our joy and freedom lasted only a few weeks. Bedbugs appeared again. Although the living bugs had been killed by the poisonous gas, their eggs had survived.

We had to admit defeat and live with the bedbugs, hoping that someday we'd build a better house with plaster walls and ceilings, and with no place to hatch our enemies.

Spanish Flu and a New Baby

In the winter of 1918-1919, Spanish flu swept through our area.

For more than a week in February 1919, our whole family, including Mama (pregnant with her fourth child), lay desperately ill. Our neighbour, S.P. Lonneberg, came over two or three times a day to do chores and bring us food. He'd set the food outside and holler anxiously through our closed door, "How are you?"

Some days we were so weak that we could hardly answer Mr. Lonneberg's call. He didn't dare enter our house for fear of catching the flu and taking it back to his family. We all needed him to be well and healthy.

Too sick to make the trek through the snow to the outhouse, we dumped our chamber pot through the sitting-room/bedroom window, out into the snow, leaving quite a mess.

Unlike many flu victims, we all survived.

On June 4th, 1919, Mama's fourth baby, Irene, was born at home, just as the rest of us had been.

But Irene was not healthy.

All through her pregnancy, Mama had not been well. Then, of course, there had also been those terrible days with the Spanish flu. Yet Mama had not seen a doctor once, not once during the entire nine months of her pregnancy. That was normal in those days.

It was twenty-five miles to the doctor and hospital in Innisfail—twenty-five miles with a team of horses through snowdrifts in the winter or muddy ruts in the summer. A trip to Innisfail meant two long days away from farm work.

Besides, who could afford the luxury of medical services? In rural areas it was just assumed that children would be born at home, with the free help of a neighbouring farm woman.

As if tormented by pain, Irene cried most of the time. She was such a pretty baby, with soft, blond hair, perfect features, and a perfectly formed body, but she never, ever gained any strength.

It didn't take long before each of us noticed that if we passed something in front of Irene's face, her beautiful grey-blue eyes didn't follow the object. Irene's eyes would follow a sound, but never a silent object. She never reached for anything.

Although we all noticed these things, no one said a word until one day when we were sitting together after supper.

Mama stroked Irene's hair, looked away, and murmured, "I'm afraid she's blind." A shiver went through me.

Irene's crying was hard on everybody's sleep, almost as persistent as the bedbugs, and we stumbled through every day's work, groggy and worried.

Mama and Papa became so desperate that they took Irene all the way to the doctor in Innisfail. "There's nothing I can do for her," said the doctor. "She'll probably grow out of it."

That autumn, Papa worked for better-established farmers, labouring for weeks for just a few dollars, so most of the chores fell on the shoulders of Mama, Arnfeld, and me.

Poor Mama. She had the worst of it. And it wasn't just the work. Day after day, night after night, Mama did her best to care for our wailing baby sister.

Arnfeld and I tried to comfort Irene, rocking her and holding her, but nothing seemed to help. And Esther? Two years old when Irene was born, Esther simply added to the crying that echoed all that year through our tiny house.

Then one morning Mama sat down by the table and rested her head in her hands. I became worried. "Mama, what's wrong?"

"I'm going to have another baby."

I just stood there shocked while she kept her head down.

In addition to dealing with a sick baby's cries of pain, Mama would somehow have to find the energy and courage to cope with her fifth pregnancy, and I sure wondered how.

OLD BIRD

Every day for two years I had been walking four miles to school and four miles back—with plenty of chores to do when I reached home.

Now in the autumn of 1919, six-year-old Arnfeld had started school. He staggered along beside me on the eight-mile round trip. At the end of each day little Arnfeld was almost sick from exhaustion.

One afternoon, when we finally reached home, Papa was gone. So was our team and wagon. "Papa went to an auction," Mama said, "to buy another horse."

We boys nodded. We knew that Papa needed more horses to clear away the bushes and trees, and to break some farmland for planting grain.

As soon as we heard the clip-clop of hooves, we raced to meet Papa. A steel-grey mare was following, tied behind the wagon.

"That's a pretty horse!" I said.

Papa stopped the wagon. "Her name is Bird."

"Bird," I whispered. The horse turned her nose to nuzzle my face. "Papa, she's not very big for working in the field."

Papa grinned. "She's for two boys to ride to school."

I buried my face in Bird's silky neck. Our very own horse. How could this be? Papa still worked for other farmers just to keep our family fed. He could not afford a horse for kids to ride to school. "Impossible," he'd said.

"Papa, thank you, thank you."

"Now," our father said, "you two boys have no excuse for coming home late to do your chores."

There was more! Papa reached into the back of the wagon and handed me a saddle. I caressed the saddle's glossy, worn leather, lifted the heavy old wooden stirrups, then quickly turned my head. But Papa had seen my tears. "Archie! Quit it!" he said, his voice stern. "Crying is for babies."

"Yes, Papa."

The next morning we rode, me in the saddle, Arnfeld bouncing behind. In the school barn, the kids crowded around, admiring our new horse. Some of the older boys even talked to me that day.

On the way home, it was Arnfeld's turn in the saddle. I bounced behind, too happy to speak. We were halfway home so soon.

Suddenly we were lying in gooey mud. "She bucked!" I looked up, shaking my head. Only our pride was hurt. Bird stood, waiting, almost smiling.

We climbed back on, and continued home, not at all relaxed, but Bird behaved perfectly.

"What happened?" Papa asked the moment we rode into the yard. He glared at our muddy clothes.

"She ... she ... she bucked us off," I said, hardly able to lift my head.

"Likely story," Papa said. "Nice, gentle horse like that. A strap awaits liars. You boys were fooling around and slid off. You'd better ride more carefully. And never lie again."

"Yes, Papa." But what if Bird bucked again the next day?

That night Arnfeld and I tramped with our father through pelting rain and howling wind, towards the barn to milk the cows. At least we could shut out the awful weather. Our barn door had a special latch that Papa had invented. My father was proud of his latch because even our friends had trouble figuring out how to open that door.

On the door's outside, all you could see was a small loop of heavy rope. If you pulled the loop's left side, the door opened; if you pulled the loop's right-hand side, the latch slid shut.

With rain pouring down her face, Bird stood watching as Papa pulled the left side of the rope loop to open the barn door. Bird tried to follow us and the cows into the warm barn, but Papa closed the door and pulled the loop to lock her out.

While we were squirting milk into the pails, the door suddenly opened, and in walked Bird.

"That's funny," said Papa. "She must have been chewing on the rope. Just happened to pull the left side with her teeth."

He chased Bird back into the rain, then pulled the cord to lock her out. Almost immediately the door swung open again, and one soaking-wet horse walked casually into the barn. "How on earth!" said Papa, his eyes wide.

The barn was already crammed with cows, people, milk stools, and pails. There was no room for a horse. "Get out, you Old Bird."

Papa chased her into the rain, pulled the loop to lock the door, and stomped back to milk his cow.

Again Bird opened the door and sauntered into the barn, letting in the howling wind and the wet night air. Papa got up, yelling, and flung his milk stool at Bird. She leaped aside, but the stool bounced hard off her shoulder. It really hurt, you could tell. The little horse scrambled from the barn.

Within seconds Bird opened the barn door again. But this time she just peeked tauntingly through the door until Papa got so angry that he flung his milk stool again. Bird stepped aside, calmly watched the stool go flying past, and then sauntered into the barn.

Papa stomped into the rain, muttering, to retrieve his stool. Arnfeld and I tried not to laugh.

Twice more that night Bird performed this trick until she had Papa trained not to throw his milk stool. He had to give up and let her in the crowded barn so he could at least keep the door shut against the cold and rain.

Before Arnfeld and I went to bed, Papa came into the house, announcing that he had created a different design for latching that barn door. This latch, he declared, could still be opened from both outside and inside, but only by humans.

The next morning Papa showed us the new latch. It was even trickier than before, a clever lock with a rope and lever. Bird stood watching.

"I got you beat, Old Bird." Papa laughed and let the cows into the barn for their morning's milking. "You boys stay outside to see what Old Bird does when she finds that she can't open the door."

As soon as Papa closed the barn door, Bird used her teeth in the way Papa had just used his hands. In a moment she had that door open.

After breakfast Arnfeld and I rode Bird to school, praying that she wouldn't buck us off. The horse behaved perfectly. She trotted home that afternoon, obeying our every command. It was hard to believe she'd ever bucked. "Just something strange happened yesterday," I said. "She'll never buck again."

Arnfeld smiled. "Bird's the best horse in the world."

When we arrived home, Papa had contrived a different lock from a bent nail, a rope, and two pieces of wood. But in a couple of minutes, Bird opened the door and came in to visit. "I'll get you," Papa muttered.

The next morning was Friday. We rode peacefully towards

school, when suddenly Bird lifted both back legs ever so gently, and down slid two boys, onto the wet grass. "She bucked again," said Arnfeld, tears flooding his eyes.

Neither of us was hurt, but fresh grass stains covered our clothes. What would Papa—and Mama—say? They could afford only one set of school clothes for each of us, and grass stains didn't come out easily. Papa would punish us. He'd say we'd been fooling around or maybe even fighting. He'd never believe Bird had bucked. Or worse, what if he did?

Bird stood grinning as though this was all a wondrous joke. We scrambled back on, and the little horse didn't buck again that day.

When we reached home Papa was smiling, eager to show off his brand-new invention for latching the barn door—until he noticed grass stains on his sons' pants and shirts. He scowled. "That horse. She really does buck, doesn't she?"

We stared at the ground.

"Answer me," Papa said.

We couldn't look up. "Yes," I finally said, "but she doesn't buck very hard."

Papa put his hands on his hips. "She's headed back to the next auction. And if I can't find another school horse, you can walk."

"No, Papa, please."

That night, when Bird opened the barn door's brand-new latch, Papa raised his fist. "That does it. Old Bird, you're leaving!"

The next morning, Saturday, Papa said, "That stupid Old Bird can help pull the plough today. I'm going to hook her up with the other horses. I'll get *something* from her before she goes back to the auction."

"You remember she's a small horse," said Mama. "Don't go overworking her just because you're mad. You can't expect her to pull like the big horses."

"She'll work. I'll make her work, don't you worry."

"If you kill her working, you won't even get your money back from her."

Speechless with dread, Arnfeld and I watched Papa fling the heavy harness on Bird, hook her with the two big horses to the plough, then stand behind the three animals, holding the plough handles. "Gid-up," Papa yelled.

Bird leaned into the harness and pulled. The plough moved forward before the other two horses had even tightened their traces. Bird kept pulling, her muscles straining, her hooves digging into the dirt. Papa tramped behind, steering the plough, his eyes wide.

Around and around, the plough sliced through the heavy ground, Bird pulling with just as much force as our big draft horses.

When Papa finally stopped the horses, we ran to hug Bird's sweating neck. "Papa, now can we keep her? Can't we, Papa?"

"Never seen anything like it," Papa said. "She sure can work. Such a small horse, that Old Bird." Papa took his hat off, wiping his forehead, shaking his head in disbelief. "She sure can work."

That evening, when he finally did manage to design a barn door latch that Bird couldn't open, Papa seemed quiet and almost disappointed as we milked the cows in peace.

From that day on, Old Bird worked for Papa in harness—on evenings, Saturdays, and school holidays, pulling with as much determination as the best draft horse in the countryside.

As a school horse, Bird continued to perform her bucking trick once in a while without ever consulting her riders. She'd lift both back legs just enough to send us sliding down, then stand waiting to continue the journey. But no more was ever said about selling Old Bird.

STARVING CATTLE

"Drop it!" we heard Mama shouting one Saturday morning in early April, 1920. Papa, Arnfeld, and I all dashed outside, leaving baby Irene crying in her cradle and three-year-old Esther playing in her highchair.

There, in front of the house, we saw our very pregnant mother chasing a cow. The cow was running with our housebroom in her mouth, chewing the straw at one end.

We all charged. The poor animal dropped the broom and plunged away through deep snow, bellowing, to join the rest of our scrawny cows. Mama picked up what was left of the broom. "Chewed right down to the handle!" she muttered.

Papa said, "That broom shouldn't have been left outside with all these starving cows around. There won't be any money for a new broom, I can tell you that."

Back into our log house we tramped. Within a few minutes all of our cattle were standing at the kitchen window, snow up to their bellies, staring with longing at Mama's geranium plants, bawling to us for food.

It had been terrible, that winter of 1919 to 1920. From the middle of October, deep snow had covered the ground, a winter without even one day of the warming chinook winds that usually blew in at least every month or so. Not this year. Not in our area.

To make matters worse, the previous summer had produced very little rain, so even the dried-out sloughs had grown almost no grass to be cut for the winter's hay.

It was April now, and hay, if you could get it, was selling for the unbelievable price of one hundred dollars a ton. Many farmers' cattle were starving to death. We had rationed our grain and our meagre supply of slough hay as much as possible to keep our cows alive. Now there was no grain, and only a few strands of hay left for the next day or so.

At lunch-time our cows were still staring through the window at the geranium plants, bawling constantly.

At the end of the meal, Papa slammed his fist on the table, bouncing the dishes. "Only six acres of cleared land! It's nothing. How am I supposed to grow anything on six acres?"

Papa seemed to be yelling right through the window at the cows. "We own 160 acres. What good does it do for us to have 160 acres when 154 of those acres are covered with bushes and trees?

"We're out of oats." Papa got up and paced the floor. "We're out of barley. The last wisp of hay will be gone tomorrow. Then our cows will die. This is wickedness. I have to clear more land next summer."

Mama said, "But everybody's cows around here are starving this winter."

Papa spun to face her. "Then everybody needs to clear more land. A farmer has to raise enough grain and hay for his animals. Besides, we need to raise extra grain and hay to sell to get some money."

"You can't clear land by yourself."

"Archie could help me."

"Archie is nine years old." Mama's face set hard. "It's bad enough how much he has to do helping me look after the farm when you're away working all the time."

"That's the point, woman. This is crazy. Me out working for other farmers just to get a few cents." He looked up at the bellowing cows. "This summer—if summer ever comes—I'm going to clear more land somehow, and that's that."

He pushed his fists together. "In the meantime, how are we going to get through this bloody winter? If only we had sold the yearling calves in October. Stupid idea it was to keep them over the winter to fatten. Fatten? Now we'll have skeletons for sale. We've got to get these cattle some hay or grain."

"Right," said Mama. A wistful twinkle came to life somewhere in her grey-blue eyes. "It would be pretty hard to find enough housebrooms to feed them all." Arnfeld giggled and Papa scowled.

The next day was Sunday. Driving our team home after church, Papa sounded much happier. "I was talking to Martin Heinsen. He has some oat sheaves we can buy."

"But Papa," Mama protested, "you know the price of oat sheaves these days. At least twenty-five cents each! Can you imagine how many dollars it would cost for enough to feed our cows even one week?"

"Martin says we don't have to pay him until we can afford to— even if it takes years!"

"That's wonderful. No, *he's* wonderful!"

For once Papa didn't argue.

Arnfeld and I rode the eight miles north with Papa and the team of horses to the Heinsens' place, pulling our big bobsled. My little brother and I helped load the oat sheaves on the bobsled, then perched on top of the bouncy sheaves, thinking we would enjoy the ride home.

A couple of miles away from the Heinsen farm, a dozen or so starving cows appeared from nowhere. Bawling, they attacked our sheaves.

"Keep them off," yelled Papa.

We waved our arms, we shouted, but those cattle had no fear. All they could think of was feed!

Papa urged the horses to a fast trot. Still the cows ran with us, bellowing, their flabby udders swinging, their frantic mouths yanking at our oat sheaves.

Arnfeld grabbed the pitchfork and waved it around. The pitchfork was bigger than Arnfeld, so I took it to wave at the cows. Still they kept grabbing our sheaves.

"Hit them!" cried Papa.

It really hurt me to clobber starving animals whose only crime was to try to eat! But I had to. We needed this feed for our cattle. I had to hit those cows hard with the back of the pitchfork, I had to smash them on their bawling faces.

The robber cows bellowed and came at us again. Over and over I had to hit them. A tine of the fork poked one of the cows in her eye. I winced, but had to keep on hitting.

The miles home seemed like forever, the big bobsled lurching and swaying, the cows bawling and coming at us with their open, desperate mouths, Papa whipping the tired horses to make them pull faster.

At last those cows gave up the chase and we reached home with most of our precious load.

The oat sheaves lasted our cattle only a couple of weeks. It was nearly the end of April and still spring had not come. All day and all night, our cattle bawled again from hunger. Out into the woods they trudged, fighting the deep snow to chew on poplar branches.

One morning Papa and I found our oldest cow lying in the woods, too weak to get up.

Pushing, pulling, prodding, Papa tried to help her stand, but she had lost her will to live.

"Archie, run home. Fast. Get a pail of potatoes."

A nine-year-old boy couldn't run fast carrying a bucket of potatoes, especially dragging them through waist-high snow, but somehow I got back there in time. Smelling food, the cow opened her eyes, slowly lifted her head, buried it in the pail, then started gobbling.

In a couple of minutes the cow had emptied the pail. She looked up at us as if to say thanks, then summoned the strength to stand again.

On the way home, wading through the snow, Papa muttered, "It's no good, animals starving like this. I've got to clear more land this summer or give up farming."

GRUB-AXE AND YELLOW JACKETS

Normally in our area of central Alberta, the snow cover would be gone—at least temporarily—sometime in April, or maybe even towards the end of March.

Not in the spring of 1920. On the 11th of May, snow still blanketed the countryside around Dickson, snow three feet deep. The cattle were hysterical from hunger.

On that evening, a warm breeze finally blew in from the southwest. All the next day it continued to blow.

By May 13th, you could almost watch the surface of the snow dropping as it turned to slush.

Within a couple of days we saw the ground for the first time in seven months. I found it hard not to cry at the miracle of green grass blades pushing their way through the mud.

By the 26th of May, Papa was out planting the crop in our only field, our tiny patch of six cleared acres surrounded by 154 acres of bushes and trees.

One day in June, Papa came home from Dickson with a strange instrument. Mounted on a three-foot-long wooden handle, was a huge, double-headed piece of steel.

"What is it?" I asked eagerly, not dreaming that within hours I'd be wishing I had never seen such a tool.

"It's a grub-axe. For clearing land." Papa pointed to the four-inch steel hoe that formed one side of the head. "This part is sharpened at the end to claw dirt away from a bush or tree root."

Then pointing to the long, narrow steel blade that formed the opposite side, Papa said, "This part is sharpened all the way along for chopping roots."

I lifted the heavy beast of a tool, and by that afternoon was taking my turn with Papa to chop at the smaller bushes: willow, dogwood, wild rose. My back burned with pain, but I didn't dare cry or complain. After all, I was almost ten years old.

All that summer, in every spare moment, Papa and I worked at clearing land. The trees and big bushes had to be yanked out by the horses using a chain and two pulleys. But before our horses could pull the trees, Papa or I would have to swing that grub-axe, over and over and over again, our muscles in agony as we tried to bare the roots and cut around them.

Papa would hook the chain high around a tree, the horses would put their shoulders hard to the harness, and hopefully the tree would be extracted, like some monstrous tooth, with most of its root intact. Often, though, the tremendous strain of pulling broke some part of the harness or rig. Good thing Papa could fix harness.

The pile of yanked-out brush and trees grew higher, until finally we had a patch of new land about the size of a garden, cleared and ready to be "broken" by its first ploughing.

I watched Papa when he began breaking the new land with our three horses and a heavy plough. Trudging behind, Papa wrestled with the plough to guide it in the new furrow. Roots, sliced through by the plough, whipped back sharply against his ankles.

Around the new patch of land, Papa ploughed, cutting through grass and roots, exposing black earth to sunlight.

Suddenly the plough jerked to a stop, horses rearing, harness snapping.

I raced over. "Papa, what happened?"

"Grab the horses! The plough's caught on something."

I tried to calm the horses while Papa hacked around the plough with the grub-axe. "It's a root," he puffed. "But it's charred and as hard as rock."

Finally Papa chopped the root free and lifted the thing, like a huge black snake. "An old spruce root. Must have been partly burned ages ago in some forest fire. It's been dried and weathered for years."

We took the sweating horses home, and Papa spent hours fixing harness. "I'm worried there might be more of those old charred spruce roots under that ground," he told Mama. "It could be mighty slow breaking this land."

How right he was!

A few minutes more of ploughing and it happened again. Luckily the jolt didn't break the harness. After we hacked out the ebony-hard root, Papa started the horses again. But the third time they jerked to a stop, another piece of harness snapped.

The next day my father tried ploughing again. He had barely started, when, as if from nowhere, a cloud of angry wasps filled the air behind the plough and attacked him.

Yelling, he slapped the reins hard on the horses' rumps. They lunged forward, pulling Papa out of the stinging cloud, so he kept on ploughing. But on the next round, as he and the horses came to the same spot, there it was again. That cloud of yellow wasps!

They attacked, and the horses, crazed with pain and terror, leapt ahead, snorting.

Suddenly the plough jerked to a stop. One of those old charred spruce roots! Horses and harness scattered in all directions. Papa lay sprawled on the ground until the yellow, buzzing cloud settled on him. He started to run, hollering, tripping, slapping wasps, jumping up, falling, yelling, running.

Papa threw himself into the water trough. Water sloshed out on the dusty ground. The yellow crowd of wasps buzzed and hovered over the water, then gradually dispersed, while I watched, totally helpless.

Papa emerged from the dirty water, moaning, holding his head, covered with welts.

That evening our neighbour, S.P. Lonneberg, sat sympathizing with Papa. "They're called yellow jackets, those wasps," he said. "And they are one of the curses of breaking land around here."

"But where did they come from?" Papa asked. "All of a sudden they were just there. I didn't see any nest and I wasn't even beside any trees."

Mr. Lonneberg shook his head. "Yellow jackets make their nests in the ground, just below the surface. You tore their nest with the plough. That was bad enough, but on the next round, the horses stepped into their torn nest, and those wasps were really ready for you."

Mama wrung cold water from a towel, dabbed it with a paste of baking soda, then spread it gently on Papa's swollen neck and scalp. "Mr. Lonneberg," she asked, "how long will these wasp welts last?"

"Quite a few days," said Mr. Lonneberg. "And it's going to take your poor old husband many hours to fix his harness and rigging again." He turned to Papa. "You were unlucky to hit one of those old rock-hard spruce roots at the same time you happened to be racing yellow jackets. But it happens. Clearing and breaking land is terrible business. Hard on the man and hard on the horses."

"I guess a person's lucky if he can break more land than equipment," said Papa, pulling his swollen face into a grin.

Mr. Lonneberg smiled. "You're going to be all right, Mr. Morck."

Out of the Woods

Papa and I managed to clear and break only three acres of our homestead that summer of 1920. Three acres added to the six acres that had already been cleared by the first homesteader who had given up.

And even after we cleared and broke those three acres, they were by no means ready for seeding. Tree roots stuck up everywhere, entangled all along the furrows. First we had to loosen the web of roots with a root harrow, a set of enormous steel teeth fastened to a heavy platform, drawn by as many horses as possible. Some of the neighbours owned eight horses, but we had only four by then, including Old Bird, so they just had to do their best.

Papa balanced on the platform of the root harrow as it jerked, jolted, and tore through the knotted roots. Every few minutes Papa had to let the horses stop for breath. The horses became so tired that I didn't even need to hold them. I patted their lathered necks, my heart aching for them.

Then came the worst part for us humans. Roots had to be yanked out by hand. Mama, Arnfeld, and even Esther (now three years old) joined in on this awful job. Beside the field, our two little baby sisters, Irene and Thora, lay crying, wrapped in blankets in two wooden apple boxes, while the rest of us all spent hours pulling roots. Thousands and thousands of roots. One by one.

You grabbed a root, but the more you pulled, the longer that piece of root became, soil rippling away, until you reached a point where the end of the root wouldn't leave the ground and what you held had to be chopped off with an axe. Over and over again, you pulled roots as far as you could, and chopped them off. Pull, pull, pull, pull, chop. Pull another, pull, pull, pull, pull, chop.

We flung the roots into piles, piles that grew and grew, but still there were more roots to be pulled.

Picking roots was even more back-breaking, tiring, and tedious than the next job on the agenda: trying to remove every rock from our new field. After total exhaustion from days of pulling roots, we had to bend over for days more, picking rocks out of the dirt, flinging them into big piles.

Using the horses, Papa hauled the roots and rocks to the edge of the new field to join the immense piles of uprooted trees and bushes.

Those enormous heaps of torn-out trees, bushes, and roots had to be burned. For many days, Papa and I tended the cracking, roaring flames, as we tried to get rid of the piles of brush. Covered with ashes, sweat, and grime, eyes and lungs burning from the smoke, I'd look up at Papa and wonder why he'd ever left the prairies for this crazy woodlands homestead.

Then the soil had to be levelled with a discer, actually a set of rotating steel discs, pulled by our faithful horses. Then our horses had to drag another harrow with smaller teeth to smooth down the soil.

Winter arrived. With great anticipation we looked forward to spring and planting more land.

But when the next spring arrived, we tried working our new land, and were dismayed to find that thousands more roots had surfaced. So before planting, we had to spend days picking roots all over again. "Breaking land takes a strong back and a weak mind," said Papa.

At last, the new land was ready for seeding with its first crop. I followed when Papa drove the horses and seeder out, and sat under a tree to watch.

Just as the first barley seeds slid into the new ground, Papa stopped the horses. He bent down, picked up a handful of the rich, black soil, and let it trickle out between his calloused fingers. It was probably just the sun reflecting, but I almost thought I saw tears in Papa's tired, squinting eyes.

GOODBYE, LITTLE SISTER

The morning of July 24th, 1920, was chilly, so Mama opened the oven door of our wood-burning cookstove. "Archie, let's get some heat in the kitchen," she said, "before we bathe these babies."

On the open oven door Mama set the basin, and pulled a chair beside it. I could hear Arnfeld and Esther laughing and playing outside our log house. I was ten, old enough and strong enough to help with nearly anything by now.

"We'll do Thora first." Mama held the tiny, squirming character on her lap, and began to bathe her, dipping and squeezing a soft square of white flannelette, wiping it over Thora's firm, pink skin.

"Here, Archie, you dry her off and dress her." Mama handed Thora to me. "I'd better tend to Irene now."

The contrast seemed too sharp: healthy, strong Thora, four weeks old, wriggling on my lap, and fourteen-month-old Irene lying limp on Mama's arm.

Stroking the tiny, frail chest with the cloth, Mama sighed, "Poor, dear little girl."

Irene was so beautiful, with her blond hair and huge blue eyes, but lately she looked worn and weary; sometimes she seemed almost ancient. Her crying had become a part of our lives, but for the past few days she had been strangely quiet.

It had been a hard fourteen months. Irene had been born ill. We mostly blamed Irene's condition on the Spanish flu that had ravaged all of us, including Mama, who had been in the final months of her pregnancy with Irene.

Now Irene was over a year old. What would happen with her life and with ours? The dark circles under Mama's eyes seemed to grow larger every day. I looked down at baby Thora. One month old and so full of life. And to think that Irene hadn't yet gained enough strength to raise her head.

Mama finished bathing Irene, wrapped her in a blanket, and held the baby to her chest. "I'll sit here for a while by the stove to warm her up."

A minute or so later, Mama took a sharp breath. "Irene." She patted the baby. "Irene."

"Mama, what's wrong?" I asked, but hardly dared to hear.

"Her breathing. It doesn't seem right. Seems so weak." She bent her face to the tiny child. "Archie, put Thora down. Run and call Papa."

I laid Thora on the bed and dashed to the door. Mama stopped me with her tears. "Never mind."

She carried Irene, still wrapped in the blanket, and laid her down, oh, so gently, beside Thora on her bed.

When Mama turned and put her arm around me, somehow it seemed that Mama was leaning on *me* for strength. But I never felt so weak in all my life. Ten years old suddenly felt very young.

We walked to the barn where Papa was cleaning out the stalls. Esther and Arnfeld stopped their playing and followed us in. My ears roared with pressure as I heard Mama's soft words, "Papa, God has taken Irene home."

Papa stood still for a second, then started walking to the house. We followed, a silent parade.

Looking down at the tiny form, Papa said, "It's for the best, I guess. She never would have been able to have a normal life." But a deep sob shook his large frame, and tears began to trickle down his rough, unshaven cheeks.

Years later, Mama told Esther, "That was the only time I ever saw your father cry. It made me love him in a way I never knew before."

Head and shoulders bent, Papa headed through the trees towards our nearest neighbours, the Lonnebergs, who lived half a mile away. Mama, Arnfeld, Esther, and I huddled together in the kitchen, crying.

The roaring in my ears became a hot, sore tightness in my throat as I cried until I felt drained and empty. But still my tears kept flowing. I had watched Irene suffer so helplessly all her short life, had loved her through my agony of watching. There seemed to be no sense in her tragic life and death.

Why did she live? Why was she created? Just to suffer, and then to die? What was the meaning of her existence on earth? Did God make this all happen? Or did the devil? It all seemed so awful and so pointless, almost cruel. Would anybody on purpose create even a house or a box or a toy to be defective, then just turn around and destroy it?

Mrs. Lonneberg came hurrying over with a few of her many children. "Oh, Mrs. Morck." She put her arm around Mama and held her. "I'm going to make you a cup of coffee."

She hugged us children. "Your little sister won't have to suffer anymore. She'll get to live in Heaven." The Lonneberg children started crying, too.

Within minutes, Mrs. Lonneberg set a cup of coffee in front of Mama. "S.P. took your husband to talk to Pastor Andersen. Then they'll go see Uncle John."

"Uncle John." That was John Pedersen, an uncle to no one in our community, but a good friend to all.

Because Mr. Lonneberg was a carpenter as well as a farmer, he would make Irene's coffin, as he always did when anyone in the community died. And Uncle John, once a tailor in Denmark, would decorate the coffin and prepare her body to be buried. I knew that all of this would be done without any charge, as it always was when anyone in our community died, without the grieving family ever having to ask that anything be done.

"You're such wonderful people—all around us," whispered Mama.

Mrs. Lonneberg rubbed Mama's hand against her own cheeks as she said, "That's what we're here for, isn't it?"

That evening Uncle John arrived at our home with the tiny coffin. I could hardly believe that Uncle John and Mr. Lonneberg, with their large hands, calloused from farm work, could possibly have made anything so incredible. White satin, padded and scalloped, covered the outside of the coffin, trimmed with polished oak. Inside the coffin, pleated and ruffled quilting made of pure white silk shimmered, with pink bows, as small as rosebuds, around the edges.

Uncle John's enormous hands lifted our sister Irene as though she were a tiny, hurt bird, placed her in the coffin, then gently closed the lid so we couldn't see her anymore. We all started crying again.

Uncle John put a hand on Esther's shoulder, and said to us, "Don't be so sad. Now the angels are taking your little sister to Heaven. Now she'll be with God." I looked up at Uncle John, his dark, curly hair framing his kind, loving face, and I believed that he truly understood our grief.

After Uncle John left, our family remained in the sitting-room/bedroom, with the coffin in the middle of the room, on the trunk that Papa had brought from Denmark so many years before.

Suddenly three-and-a-half-year-old Esther walked over to the coffin, reached up, and lifted the lid.

Papa grabbed her, slapped her hands, and yelled, "No!"

Esther was shattered. She sobbed, "I just wanted to see the angels." And she would not be comforted.

When Mama put her to bed, Esther was still crying. "I just wanted to see the angels, Mama. And Papa hit me. Irene was still there. Uncle John said the angels took her to Heaven. But she was still there."

I could not stand the idea of attending the funeral, of having my school friends and everyone else watch me cry. In those days the whole school would be closed for a funeral of any member of the community.

"Mama, Papa," I said the next morning, "please could I stay home and take care of Thora when you go to the funeral? I'm ten. I could do it. Please."

"Archie, you have to go," said Papa. "You have to go to your sister's funeral."

I wanted to explain to them why I couldn't go. But I just stood there shaking my head.

"All of your classmates will be there," said Papa. "They'll wonder why you aren't there."

Mama nodded to Papa, and then she hugged me very tightly. "Yes, Archie, you could stay home to take care of Thora. We'll ask Tina to come over to help you look after Thora. Arnfeld and Esther, if you want, you can stay home too."

Tina! Oh, good! We loved Tina. S.P. Lonneberg's eldest daughter, her name was really Mrs. Katherina Adamsen, but we always called her Tina.

Before the funeral, Tina arrived, and then Mr. and Mrs. Lonneberg drove over with their team and democrat wagon. Papa lifted the tiny coffin up onto the democrat and covered it with a blanket. Then he helped Mama climb into the wagon, and sat beside her. It was the first time I'd seen Papa sit with his arm around Mama.

We children cried as they drove away, down the lane.

"Come," said Tina softly to us, "let's go walk out in the trees and pick a bouquet of wildflowers to put on the table for your mother when she comes home. Tiger lilies, bluebells, shooting stars, maybe we'll even find some wild roses still blooming."

THE SUNDAY AFTER

Every Sunday morning at 10 o'clock, the big bronze bell in the tower of Bethany Lutheran Church would ring for several minutes, calling us from our homestead, calling across the four miles from Dickson.

When the bronze bell rang the first time, our family had to be on our way, because in one hour the bell would ring again, at eleven o'clock, time for the church service to begin.

Only when the weather was incompatible with human survival would we be allowed to stay home from church. But this was the end of July, a beautiful summer day, and I knew there was no point in asking if I could stay home from church the first Sunday after Irene's funeral. How I dreaded the staring, the questions, even the friendliness.

Usually I didn't mind going to church. Quite the contrary. Especially during summer "vacation" months. After a week of heavy farm work, it seemed a treat to go to church and see my friends. But not today.

We rode in a grain box, long, narrow, and deep, made of rough wooden boards. Because it was summer, the grain box sat on a set of four wooden wheels. We called this rig a lumber wagon, and there was no support or suspension of any kind. We jiggled and swayed, all of us immersed in our own quiet thoughts.

In a few months it would be winter. Then we'd lift the grain box onto a set of sleigh runners and call the outfit a bobsled. Neither lumber wagon nor bobsled would have been good enough to take little Irene to her funeral. Mr. Lonneberg had taken her to the church in his lovely democrat buggy.

A grain box was good for hauling just about anything else, from hay to hogs, from grain to grandmothers. But not dead people. Maybe now Irene was special. After all, when she was alive, the grain box had been considered good enough for Irene, like the rest of us, to ride in.

We sat perched on board benches. Usually remnants of grain,

dust, and hay swirled all around us. But I noticed that Papa had swept out the wagon box for us this morning. Maybe her death made us a bit special as a family, too.

In one more month school would start again. Soon it would be winter. Then our team of horses would trot along smartly, warm in their thick, furry winter coats, while we huddled in the straw-filled grainbox, our bodies covered with itchy wool underwear, coats, blankets, and wool hats.

In the winter we'd heat stones and chunks of iron all night in the oven of Mama's cookstove to help warm us under the blankets while we rode in the grain box. Would Irene be warm or cold in Heaven in the winter?

Winter always seemed so long. I dreaded it. But then someday at last spring would come.

In the spring our horses would begin to shed. Despite our most vigorous currying, hair from the horses' long and shaggy coats, hair by the handful, would fly back at us in the grain box. On the way to church we'd be spitting hair from our mouths and rubbing it from our eyes. Then we'd walk into the church with our good Sunday clothes looking like old horse blankets. Just thinking about it, I giggled.

Papa looked back at me, scowling. "Archie!" was all he said, but I felt terrible. No, it wasn't right to laugh at anything, with my little sister dead.

Just as we came in sight of the church, the big bell started to ring again. Nearly eleven o'clock now.

Carl Christiansen, our storekeeper and postmaster, my good, kind friend (who sometimes gave me licorice), had donated the bell to the church many years before, and it seemed as though "Uncle Carl" was calling to me there on the lumber wagon, telling me that it would be all right to be together with everyone in church that day.

We entered the church, hugged by many people, and sat in our usual pew, with Papa at one end, then myself, Arnfeld, Esther, and then Mama holding baby Thora at the other end.

I was surprised to find that we had a visiting pastor that Sunday. The minute this pastor opened his mouth to start the sermon, it was obvious that he was a special master of what we called the "predikketone" (Danish for "preaching voice").

Pastors who used the "predikketone" talked with ordinary voice tones in everyday life but in their sermons they somehow tightened their vocal cords to sound loud and shrill, a kind of holy whine.

Beyond that, pastors using the "predikketone" had a pattern for delivering their sermons.

This visiting pastor began his sermon with a soft voice, gradually built to the loud whine, then eased back in pressure to a slow, sustained whisper. Suddenly he erupted in a dramatic, staccato scream, "I will never leave you nor forsake you." I jumped. Was that a message from Irene?

Over and over again, he repeated that scripture verse in all possible dramatic variations of the "predikketone." Although I was exhausted from the past few sleepless nights, I certainly didn't have a chance to doze off. Still, I understood little of what the pastor said.

All families of our congregation spoke Danish at home, so it was assumed that children could understand Danish sermons. But we didn't. Deep theological language was far beyond a ten-year-old, yet there was almost no attempt by any pastors in those days, visiting or otherwise, to give explanations or illustrations for young minds.

At that age, I assumed that God spoke Danish because the Bible and all of Christ's words in it were in Danish. In home devotions, church services, Sunday School, confirmation classes—anything to do with God—the only acceptable language was Danish, even though we had to speak English in our regular school classes.

The only time I had ever heard the name of God in English was in swearing. Some of the Danish immigrants who could barely express themselves in ordinary English sentences, were eloquent when it came to swearing in English.

The preacher shouted again, interrupting my thoughts. "I will never leave you nor forsake you!"

I squirmed. Papa glared at me, but didn't inflict his usual instant discipline of pulling my ear. Whether we understood a sermon or not, all of us children had to sit still in church or there would be an encounter with a piece of leather at home. But that Sunday none of us felt like misbehaving.

After the worship service, as always, Papa and Mama went to the back of the church to visit with the adults. Arnfeld, Esther, and I went to our separate Sunday School classes. My Sunday School teacher, Mrs. Laursen, hugged me, and I realized this was indeed better than staying home to cry alone.

My friends seemed so gentle, too, none of their usual friendly banter, so I took a deep breath and started to listen to Mrs. Laursen's Bible stories.

At the end of the hour, all Sunday School classes joined, as always, for the old Danish closing hymn. The last line was "Saa skal vi nok komme Hjem," which in English translates to "Then shall we all reach home."

By then it would be one o'clock, my stomach always had sharp hunger pains, and that last line usually took on a mundane but urgent meaning: "Now at last we'll be getting home—to a good meal." But this time I thought of the Heavenly home that the hymn really referred to, and wondered if my sister Irene could hear us singing about it.

That afternoon, Arnfeld and I spent hours climbing the heavily wooded hills and banks of the Red Deer River where it ran through the corner of our land. How we loved the river: our swimming pool in the summer, our ice rink in the winter, our fishing spot the whole year around.

The hills and riverbank had always been a refuge to me. I looked at the river now, trying to hold back my tears. "Hey, Archie, look what I brought," said Arnfeld. He reached into his pocket and pulled out a few tiny chunks of chicken meat that he had saved from dinner. He looked up at me for approval. "Bait," he said. "We could catch some fish for Mama." We cut slender willow sticks, and tied together pieces of cotton strings that we kept in our pockets. We used the small, plain steel, barbed hooks that we always left down by the river.

That afternoon we caught several big whitefish. I flinched to watch them struggle, to make them die. But I thought of how much happier Mama would be when we brought home the delicious fish for our whole family to eat for supper.

All Sunday afternoons came to an end too soon. We always had to go home to milk the cows. Arnfeld and I loved any Sunday afternoon, the only time of the week that we were officially allowed free time.

That Sunday afternoon after Irene's funeral stands out above all the others. And the fish that we caught that afternoon turned out to be the most delicious ever.

Remembering

For me, the strangest part about losing Irene, was how fast life returned to normal. There was always so much work to be done, so many other things to think about.

Arnfeld and I, seven and ten years old, were expected to pull our weight. I thought of Irene constantly those first few days as Arnfeld and I worked together milking cows, feeding the animals, and doing all of the other farm chores.

Would there be work to do in Heaven? I wondered

I thought of Irene as Arnfeld and I helped with the cooking, the cleaning, and the washing (even with only one baby now, there were diapers, diapers, and more diapers).

As I scrubbed the wooden floor of our two-room log house, splinters tore into my scrub cloth, a couple of splinters stabbing into my fingers. I thought of my dead sister and wondered if she felt pain anymore.

I thought of Irene when Mama, Papa, Arnfeld, Esther, and I were picking roots and rocks, and was shocked to find myself feeling almost glad that she didn't have to be there crying in her apple box at the edge of the field.

Would Irene grow in Heaven, would she eventually grow up, or would she always stay as a baby, even one hundred years from now? I never dared ask anyone any of these questions, not even Mama.

That summer, every time we went to church in Dickson, we walked over to the small mound of dirt that was Irene's gravesite, and stared down at the small wooden cross that someone had made to mark her place. Did Irene know that we were looking at her grave? Was she watching us from Heaven?

It seemed strange to me that it was only after Irene died that Mama and Papa decided to make our log house bigger by adding a two-room lumber lean-to. The new lean-to gave us two bedrooms, one for Arnfeld and me, one for Esther. Esther had to share her bedroom with Papa's leather equipment, because now that we were clearing and breaking land, Papa needed a place to do his almost-daily repair of broken harness.

But wouldn't it have been nice to have had the extra space in the sitting-room/bedroom for Mama and Papa when the babies, Irene and Thora, were sleeping in there with them? My parents mustn't have had the energy to build the lean-to when they were coping with Irene's incessant crying.

Every day of that autumn in 1920, I thought of my little sister as Arnfeld and I carried armfuls of wood and buckets of water to the house, thinking of all the diapers she didn't need anymore, all the clothes she'd never grow up to wear, of all the things she'd never get a chance to do.

Soon it was winter and we were carrying in buckets of snow to melt for washing clothes. With horror one evening, I realized that I hadn't thought of Irene once that day, maybe not even the day before.

Arnfeld and I chopped kindling, milked cows, and tramped through the snow to feed animals, and it seemed that we hardly had time to think of anything. Still, many a time I forced myself to remember my dead sister, because it seemed so wrong to forget.

Our new two-bedroom addition had absolutely no heat or insulation. I'd lie there shivering at night, especially in the early hours of the morning, wondering if Irene felt cold in her grave.

When spring came, we walked from the church over to the graveyard and saw the little wooden cross had fallen under the burden of snow. I picked it up from the mud and the melting snow, and jammed it into the ground, feeling unexplainably angry.

As the summer of 1921 wore on, we usually made the four-mile trip to Dickson a couple of times a week, but it seemed that we were always in a hurry and we went less and less often to the cemetery to see Irene's grave.

One afternoon, standing in the barn, feeding the cattle, I realized that I hadn't thought of my dead little sister for weeks. We had to keep remembering that she had lived. Surely she was born for some reason. Surely we owed it to her to at least remember that she existed.

I decided then and there that if I got to grow up and marry and have children, I would call my first daughter Irene. I'd give her my little sister's name, so that in some way her memory would keep going.

But that resolution seemed so far away, and it certainly didn't seem enough for now. There had to be something for now that I could do. Yes, there was. I looked around the barn, took out my pocket knife, and on a feed manger, in a place that I would see every day, I carved the name "Irene." Beside it I carved a tiny cross.

If anyone ever noticed that carving, I never heard about it, but I saw it there every day when I did chores.

FIVE PENNIES

In January 1922, when a kind bachelor neighbour, Carl Lorenzen, was visiting, Esther sat on his lap and chatted. Children always loved to sit on Mr. Lorenzen's lap and talk to him.

"I know how to count now," Esther said. "In one month I'll be five years old. And Arnfeld will be nine years old. In two weeks. I know lots of numbers."

Mr. Lorenzen took some coins from his pocket. "Here, Esther, show me that you know how to count. Pick out five pennies."

"One, two, three," Esther counted, "four, five."

"Very good," Mr. Lorenzen said.

Esther beamed, handing him back the pennies.

"No, they're yours," he said. "You can keep them."

In those days young children almost never had money, not even one penny. Five cents was an exciting fortune. It took quite a bit of persuasion from Mr. Lorenzen to convince Mama and Papa that little Esther should keep the pennies.

Esther was thrilled with her new treasure.

A few days later, when Papa had to go to Carl Christiansen's general store in Dickson, Esther went along, clutching her five precious pennies.

In the store, to Papa's amazement, Esther said, "I'm going to use my five pennies to buy Arnfeld a present for his birthday."

Papa was very pleased with Esther's generosity, and praised her. He helped her choose a bag of peppermints for her brother. They cost exactly five cents.

Our family almost never had enough money for candies, so Esther was proud to be able to buy such a birthday present. Back home, she hid the gift in her little lean-to bedroom, in the bottom dresser drawer, beneath her stockings and underwear.

The next morning, Esther went back into her bedroom to check on the candies. Yes, the peppermints were still there. They looked so delicious. Esther desperately needed to taste one, but they were for Arnfeld, and Papa had told her that the bag said it contained fifty peppermints. It would be no good if Arnfeld counted them and found one missing.

Esther thought of the perfect solution. Just open the package, suck on one peppermint for a moment, then put it back. So Esther did enjoy the wonderful taste—for a little while—and then put the candy back.

The next day, Esther again craved peppermint. But she couldn't suck the same candy or she would wear it down to an obviously smaller size. She could, however, taste a different one.

Each day, when the craving for peppermint became unbearable, Esther tried a new peppermint, enjoyed it for a moment, then put it back.

At last came the day of Arnfeld's birthday. With great pride, Esther presented her brother with the bag of peppermints. "Happy birthday, Arnfeld. Peppermints! I bought them with my own five pennies. There's fifty peppermints, a whole bag full."

Overwhelmed, eyes wide with joy, Arnfeld thanked Esther. But his joy turned to shock as he reached into the bag to take one of his peppermints. The candies were not only gooey and stuck together, they were grubby from Esther's repeated handling.

Puzzled for a moment, Arnfeld looked at Esther, then his face showed total disgust as he realized what must have happened. He flung the bag of peppermints at his little sister, shouting, "Keep your sticky, dirty old candy." He ran out of the room crying.

Esther bawled, too, shattered at Arnfeld's lack of appreciation for her great generosity.

And no one ever told Carl Lorenzen what happened with the five pennies that he'd given to Esther.

ESTHER RIDES A SHEEP

Whether Arnfeld and I were working or playing around the farm, Esther loved to tag along. We'd tease our cute little sister until she would run to Mama crying, "The boys are teasing me."

Mama would laugh and say, "So why don't you just leave the boys alone?" Esther always dried her tears and came back for more.

Arnfeld and I enjoyed riding the calves, pretending to be cowboys. When Papa bought two sheep, we rode them, too, clinging to their long wool for support.

After one rainy summer weekend, the barnyard oozed mud and soggy manure. On Monday afternoon when the rain finally stopped, it was too muddy to work, so Arnfeld and I decided to ride the sheep. Sheep slipped around in the muck, making for very exciting rides.

Five-year-old Esther made her usual rounds and stood watching us as we rode the sheep. "Hey, Esther," we called, "how come you're wearing your frilly pink dress? Sunday was yesterday. Remember, we went to church? Today is Monday. When you have only one fancy dress, too bad you're not smart enough to know what day it is."

Esther tossed her blond braids. "Mama is expecting some ladies for tea. She told me I had to wear my Sunday dress."

"Maybe you're so ugly that Mama has to try to make you look good somehow in front of her friends. See, she braided your hair real fancy. She probably is so ashamed of you that she has to dress you up and fix your hair so you don't look too scary."

Off went Esther wailing. We laughed. Within minutes she was back. "Hey, Archie and Arnfeld," Esther called, "can I ride the sheep, too?"

"No. You'd get your fancy pink dress all dirty if you fall. Mama would get real mad."

"Mama never gets mad. Hardly ever."

"Well, this would be one time. If you fell in the mud and the gooey manure with your one good dress, she'd get mad. Honest, she would."

"I won't fall. I hang on tight. You know I won't fall."

"It's slippery. The sheep slide around a lot."

"I'll hang on real tight. I won't fall. Please let me."

"Mama wouldn't want you to be riding sheep in your one and only Sunday dress."

"I won't tell Mama. I won't. Please."

"Mama would sure find out that you'd been riding sheep if you fell off and showed up all covered in muck. You'd see that she could get mad at you."

"I won't fall."

"You can ride the sheep another day—when you're back to looking like your normal ugly self." To our surprise Esther didn't run off crying this time.

"Please, guys."

We sighed. "OK, you're the one who will get in trouble."

Arnfeld and I led one of the sheep from the dung to some clean grass at the edge of the pasture, held the animal by its thick wool, and lifted Esther in her pretty pink dress onto its back. "Now, remember, this is your idea, Esther. Hang on tight! Ready?"

She nodded.

We let go. The animal bolted, not on the grass, but back into the corral, along the edge of the muck, rubbing hard against a gate, squeezing Esther's leg. Esther screamed. She let go of the wool to grab at the gate.

The sheep darted out from underneath Esther, and PLOP! One little girl and pink frilly dress landed in the greenish-brown manure and mud.

Her beautiful braids and face surfaced, covered with gooey muck mixed with tears. Esther went running to the house, and of course that was just the time the ladies had arrived for tea.

Our usually good-natured mother was furious. Arnfeld and I were not surprised that Mama was angry at Esther. But what we two boys could hardly believe was that Mama was angry also at Arnfeld and me. In fact she was even more angry at us than she was at Esther. "But we didn't do anything wrong," we said. "This was all Esther's idea. She insisted that we let her ride the sheep." The more we tried to explain, the more angry Mama became at us two boys.

"This just isn't like our mother," said Arnfeld. "I can't figure it out."

LICORICE

A visitor to our home happened to mention that Carl Christiansen had started buying hair from horses' manes and tails at his general store in Dickson. "He'll give you pretty good money for it, too," the man said. "The horse hair is sold to a dealer in Innisfail, for couch stuffing and violin bows and linings of suit collars."

"Horses need their manes and tails for protection against flies and cold," said Papa. "I won't be allowing any of our horses to be cropped."

The next morning Arnfeld and I took a jack-knife and cropped our horse Old Bird a bit, only a bit so that Papa wouldn't notice. And sure enough, when we brought the hair from Old Bird's mane and tail to "Uncle Carl"'s store, he gave us a licorice pipe and a licorice stick.

Arnfeld and I went home and cropped our work horses as much as we dared, for more licorice. Using our jackknives, we cut the hair as ragged as possible so that Papa would never guess.

Any more cutting and we knew that Papa would notice, so we started pulling the long hairs right out of the horses' manes and tails, but there was a limit to how much hair we could pull out without making the manes and tails look too thin.

Frantic for more licorice, we walked the edges of the pasture, collecting all of the tail hair that had pulled out on fence wires and posts where the horses had been rubbing.

Over the next few days, all the other boys at school cropped their horses for licorice, too. Everyone cut and pulled as carefully as possible, because we knew that most of our parents would not approve of horses with skimpy manes and tails, neither in the cold, nor in the fly season.

When our supply of hair ran out, one of the boys suggested we could carefully crop the horses that the girls and the little kids rode to school. They wouldn't notice.

That noon, most of us boys went to the school barn, cropped horses that did not belong to us, strolled to the Dickson general store, and enjoyed the resulting licorice, pleased with our great idea.

But we had been a little too ardent in our cropping that day. The girls and the little kids certainly did notice. They were not pleased when they went to the school barn that evening to get their mounts. And their parents were furious when they arrived home.

We all got into a lot of trouble. Many of us had stinging encounters with straps at home.

Still, our desire for licorice had become insatiable. "There must be a way to get more licorice," said one of the boys as we were lounging around one afternoon recess in the school barn.

Just then a hen cackled from one of the two hay mangers that ran along opposite sides of the barn. The hen must have laid an egg. Two or three more hens were scratching around in the school barn, too. These hens belonged to "Uncle Carl," whose chickens often wandered into the nearby school barn, and sometimes laid eggs in the mangers.

"Hey, guys," said one of the boys, "I know how we can get more licorice." He grinned. "Eggs. Everybody knows that Uncle Carl will trade produce from farms for things from his store, right?"

"Right!" another boy said. "We bring Carl Christiansen some eggs that we just happen to have found in the school barn."

"Yes," chimed in another. "And we don't have to *lie* about where we got them. We just don't have to say anything about their origin."

"Carl Christiansen will just assume that we brought them from our own hens at home," another boy said. "Mama often brings eggs in. Everybody's parents do. He'd never dream that we'd be bringing in his own eggs."

"And we won't be doing anything that wrong," I said, "because we won't be lying. Besides, his hens didn't lay them in his barn. They laid them on school property. So he probably wouldn't even have had these eggs anyway. They'd just be wasted."

We hid that first egg to wait for more to be laid. It would look suspicious to bring just one or two eggs at a time. Farmers usually brought at least a dozen eggs at once to exchange for store items. We'd have to wait until Carl's hens presented us with more eggs so that we could bring a collection of at least a few, hopefully a dozen.

No eggs appeared in the school barn mangers the next day. We didn't have much patience. Someone brought a bit of grain to school and scattered the kernels around to attract Carl Christiansen's chickens. That worked. Within a day or so, we had plenty of chickens in the barn, and within a few days we had a dozen eggs. Surely that would be enough to trade.

At noon we went to Carl Christiansen's store. The small group who had been chosen, sauntered into the store, a few eggs clutched in the hands of each one of us.

"Hi, Uncle Carl," said one of the older boys as nonchalantly as possible. "Would you like to trade a dozen eggs for some licorice?"

Uncle Carl leaned on his store counter, grinned down at the eggs clutched in our trembling hands, and chuckled. "Oh, no, boys. I don't think I could buy those eggs because I think they are *my* eggs. I'll bet you found them in the school barn."

We always wondered how he knew.

~

Christmas Is Coming

In the autumn of 1922, when our whole family was away visiting one day, skunks sneaked into the chicken coop and murdered all of Mama's chickens. Mama always financed our family's Christmas presents by raising chickens. We knew that on Christmas Eve that year there would be no Christmas presents, because there wasn't one penny extra in our family's budget.

To a Dane, Christmas is really Christmas Eve, December 24th. That's when Danes have their big Christmas meal and family Christmas celebration, and that's when Danes open their Christmas presents. December 25th was simply for church and visiting.

As the Christmas of 1922 approached, closer and closer, I wondered how it would be to have no Christmas presents this year, not even one. Maybe I could think of something to make for each member of my family so that no one would feel too disappointed. But what could a kid make? I thought and thought.

The whole Christmas season was definitely the highlight of my year, not only because of our family Christmas Eve celebrations, but also because of the church Christmas concert on the evening of December 26th.

At home, we children spent weeks making decorations for our own Christmas tree. There wasn't any money for crepe paper this year, but we threaded spruce cones to make garlands, and we cut up old catalogue pages to make paper ladders and heart-shaped baskets. We even used what sugar could be spared to create some homemade candies. We baked thousands of tiny Pebernoders—spicy Danish Christmas cookies, about the size and shape of a little fingertip.

As always, our family gathered with the whole community at the church in Dickson one evening to make decorations for the big Christmas tree at the church. It wasn't even a week now until Christmas! You could almost taste the excitement.

The adults sat at a long table to make crepe-paper flowers in splendid colours, angel ladders from tissue paper, and heart-shaped candy baskets woven from strips of shiny, coloured paper.

Older children who proved themselves careful enough were allowed to help. I was twelve, so they allowed me to make one angel ladder, my fingers clumsy with the soft tissue paper. The ladder didn't look too good, but Mama helped me fix it up. Then I ran off to play with the other kids.

When the adults had finished their cutting, weaving, and gluing, we little ones looked on, salivating, while the adults filled those woven, heart-shaped paper baskets with candies (homemade and even a few store-bought). Children were never allowed to help with this task, nor were any of us ever allowed to snitch samples.

We watched as the decorations and candy-filled baskets were packed into boxes, to be put away until the church's Christmas concert on December 26th.

To finish off the exciting evening of preparation, the choir had its final practice of Christmas carols. Listening to the magnificent carols excited me even more.

Before we went home, we all had "coffee." Whenever and wherever Danes gathered for social occasions, coffee, sandwiches, cookies, and Danish pastry were served, but Danes always referred to all of this simply as "coffee."

As always, a few days before Christmas, one of the men of the congregation cut a magnificent spruce tree, taller than any person. The next day, we all gathered at the church to decorate the tree.

This year's tree was at least ten feet high. The tree was fragrant, bushy, perfectly shaped, with balanced, tapered branches and millions of thick, silky, dark needles. "I really do think that this one is the best, most beautiful Christmas tree we've ever had," people said. But they always said that every year, with every Christmas tree.

Only the adults decorated the Christmas tree, stretching angel ladders from branch to branch, hanging the candy-laden paper baskets, attaching the spring-clip holders at the end of the spruce branches and putting a white candle into each holder.

At last the tallest man in our community stood tip-toe on a stool, arms stretched high, to crown the tree with the shining star made of gold and silver paper. Everyone gasped with admiration and excitement, then said again that this surely was the most beautiful tree we'd ever had for the church.

Again, "coffee" was served. Smelling the spruce needles, listening to the happy voices, watching the tree and its decorations, I felt so excited that I wondered how I could possibly wait until Christmas. Who cared that there would be no Christmas presents for one year?

CHRISTMAS, AFTER ALL

I still hadn't thought of any presents that I could make so that our tree at home would have at least some Christmas packages under it. Might as well just give up, I told myself. Nobody was expecting anything anyway.

Mama and Papa had made it quite clear that they had no money for any Christmas presents because the skunks had killed all of Mama's chickens, which would have paid for the gifts.

There wouldn't even be money for Mama to buy wool to knit any of us a pair of socks or mitts for Christmas, not even a pair of booties for our brand-new baby sister, Alice, born in September.

Mama didn't have a spinning machine, so she could never spin our own sheep's wool into yarn for knitting. She always just washed and carded wool from our sheep, then traded it at Carl Christiansen's store for wool yarn. This year the wool had all been traded to buy shoes, overalls, sugar, salt, and other necessities.

On the afternoon of December 24th, 1922, as always, our family put up the beautiful tree that Papa had cut. We had so much fun decorating it that I almost forgot about Christmas presents.

By the time the sun went down, the delicious, pungent smell of Danish red cabbage in its vinegar-and-sugar sauce permeated our log house. From the oven came the fabulous aroma of our best cut of roast pork.

A knock on the door. That would be Carl Lorenzen and Marius Thomsen, two of the community's bachelors invited to join our Christmas Eve celebrations. We ran to open the door. Our visitors stamped the snow off their boots and came in, cheeks rosy, eyes shining.

After the festive meal, everybody except Papa and our two visitors remained in the kitchen to do dishes.

After doing dishes, we gathered in the sitting-room/bedroom, around the fragrant spruce tree. Our homemade decorations looked just fine.

Papa read the Christmas story from Luke 2 and prayed, a long prayer that left Arnfeld, Esther, me, and especially two-year-old Thora squirming restlessly. Baby Alice slept blissfully in her cradle.

At last it was time for Mama to light the candles on the tree. We turned down the kerosene lamps, our hearts pounding with excitement as each white candle came to life.

Joining hands, we formed a circle and moved around the tree, lustily singing—off-key—every word of our beloved Danish Christmas carols, breathing deeply of the smell of candlewax and spruce, as the candlelight sparkled in our eyes, and our tall shadows danced on the walls and the ceiling.

When we ran out of carols, we blew out the candles to save them for New Year's Eve, and turned up the kerosene lamps. This was the time that we normally distributed the gifts. But, of course, the space under the Christmas tree this year was empty.

Yet suddenly, to my amazement, Mama reached behind the couch and put four small packages under the tree. Each package was wrapped in used tissue paper.

Arnfeld, Esther, Thora, and I were each handed one of the packages. Trying not to tear the paper in our excitement, we opened the packages. There was a pair of knitted mitts for each of us, all four pairs of mitts made from the same dark green wool. Laughing, Mama fitted a tiny pair of dark green booties onto Alice's wiggling feet.

Where did Mama get that wool? It looked familiar. Then it hit me. Mama had unravelled one of her own two sweaters to get wool to make new mitts for us.

Even in a good year the chickens didn't bring much money, so our Christmas presents had always been frugal, but to us they had always seemed special. Besides a new shirt or coat, hand-knit socks and mittens, there usually had been at least one toy or game for each of us from the Eaton's catalogue, and usually a twenty-five-cent doll for Esther.

This Christmas Eve, Arnfeld and I raved over our new mitts, and Mama looked grateful when we did. Two-year-old Thora, too young to remember last year's Christmas presents, was also content with her new mitts. But I could see that Esther remembered well the games and dolls from Christmas Eves past. Esther looked sad, and so did Mama whenever she glanced at her five-year-old daughter's dismal face.

In desperation, I went out to my lean-to bedroom, to the drawer under my bed in which I kept my clothes and possessions, and took out the picture from the old calendar that Mama had given to me two whole years before, when 1920 ended. She had given it to me because I loved it so much, that brightly coloured calendar picture of a little boy and a little girl with their beautiful collie dog.

Out in the kitchen I found a piece of brown paper that Carl Christiansen had used to wrap some sugar. Carefully I rolled the pretty picture, wrapped the brown paper around it, and tied the tube with a string.

Back into the living room I went. "Here, Esther," I said, handing it to my little sister. "It's another Christmas present for you."

She looked puzzled, almost suspicious. But when she opened it, her eyes lit up, and she hugged the picture to her chest.

The best part of all was the smile I got from Mama, our two guests, and, yes, from Papa, too. I felt on top of the world.

After opening our presents, we always spent the rest of Christmas Eve playing games. It didn't matter that we had no new games to play this year. Our favourite Christmas game, anyway, was played with only the spicy little Pebernoder cookies that we had baked especially for Christmas.

The adults visited while we children played with the Pebernoders, hiding the tiny cookies in our clenched hands, letting the others guess how many we had hidden, passing the handful each time onto the victor, eating the cookies as we played. So what if the Pebernoders looked a bit grubby after being hidden in our sweaty palms? We ate the little cookies until our stomachs could hold no more.

Finally it was time for Arnfeld and me to say groggy goodnights. By then it was hours past our usual bedtime. Esther had already gone to bed long before, happily clutching her new mitts and her pretty calendar picture.

Had there ever been a better Christmas Eve?

THE CONCERT

Christmas Day, 1922.

Esther, Arnfeld, Thora, and I all put on our new green mitts and felt quite dressed up for the Christmas Day church service. But we yawned because we'd gone to bed so late the night before.

No matter how tired we might be from our special Christmas Eve night, we still had to get to Dickson for Christmas Day service by eleven o'clock. Everyone in the community went to church on Christmas Day, even those few people who hadn't attended church since Easter.

At the Christmas Day service, the splendid decorated tree stood at the front of the church, its candles still not lit. The candles were never lit until the Christmas concert the next evening, December 26th.

At the Christmas Day service, as at all of our Christmas gatherings, we sang the old Danish Christmas carols with great gusto, even those of us who couldn't carry a tune in a bucket. For the Danes of Dickson, Christmas Day was a day to relax, a day between the family celebrations of Christmas Eve and the exciting Christmas concert.

At last December 26th arrived, the long-awaited night of the Christmas concert. Everyone, dressed in his or her very best, crammed into the church. For that night alone, we, the Sunday School children, had the privilege of sitting in pews set on both sides of the Christmas tree, facing the congregation.

Now at last the candles on the tree were lit, their flames dancing and sparkling in our excited eyes.

We children, in turn, cleared our throats to recite Christmas hymns, old Testament prophecies, and parts of the Christmas story, while all of our anxious parents mouthed the well-rehearsed lines.

Some children barely managed a nervous whisper; other children shouted. Some mumbled, a few whimpered, others raced through their lines, some (me included) forgot their words. But always there would be a few characters who gave perfect performances—potential auctioneers or preachers.

Next came the special music. How we all loved Fred Pedersen's violin solo! How we all loved the choir, with Fred Pedersen directing, smiling, and swinging his whole body to the music.

But neither the children who recited, nor Fred Pedersen's choir, nor any of the other performers could ever count on finishing their selection in peace.

Paper flowers on the tree inevitably caught fire from the candles. Of course, this night was no exception. People screamed and gasped as tall men rushed to crush the flames with their bare hands, while others grabbed mops and pails of water that were kept on hand for these emergencies.

The second blaze that night was one of the grandest I'd seen, reaching the danger point, people really screaming. But as always, even that blaze was brought under control by brave hands and by ample splashes of water.

After each flare-up, the Christmas concert program would continue until interrupted by the next fire on the Christmas tree.

During the closing hymn, we children wriggled with excitement, mouths watering, eyes fixed on the candy-filled woven paper baskets hanging from the tree. One of these heart-shaped paper baskets, including the candy in it, would be handed out to each child.

At last the program was over, and I held my paper basket full of candy, trying to decide which one to try first.

That wasn't all! Each person, from the toddlers to the grandparents, would receive an apple. What a treat! Each pioneer, old or young, looked forward to this apple, the only apple that most people—certainly our family—tasted all year.

What a dilemma: should I eat my apple right here, right now, or should I save it until later, maybe even for a day or so, enjoying the anticipation of that delicious, juicy flavour?

Most children, and many adults, succumbed to the temptations of instant gratification. That's what I'd always done, too, biting immediately into the apple, juice running down my chin, and within minutes the pleasure was all over. This year, I had decided, would be different. I'd save my apple for a day or so.

But I watched most of the other people crunching into their

apples, and a few seconds later, I gave in. What a flavour! Maybe next year I'd wait. Then again, maybe not.

Our family hardly went anywhere at night, so even the long ride home in the grain box seemed part of the magic. To the music of the bobsled's metal runners squeaking over the frozen snow, and the jingle of the horses' harness, I savoured what remained of my candy. Then I shoved my hands back into my new green woollen mitts, and watched the stars—God's candles, I called them—sparkling more radiantly than any candles on a tree.

HOMEMADE

Our good neighbour, S.P. Lonneberg, had a special hobby. In the long, dark winter evenings, he would knit sweaters. Beautiful sweaters. He knit them for his thirteen children, and he knit them for himself and his wife. Everyone admired Mr. Lonneberg's sweaters.

One winter evening, at the age of twelve, I asked Mama, "Someday when we get enough money for some wool, could you teach me to knit?"

Mama smiled. "Maybe when another few cream cheques come, maybe there'll be something left over after we buy groceries. Then we can get a ball of wool for you to make a pair of mitts."

Sure enough, about a month later, Mama handed me a ball of soft, grey wool. "Ready for your knitting lesson?" she asked. Out came an old pair of knitting needles for me. Under Mama's direction, I looped grey yarn onto the knitting needles, then clicking them, slowly at first, and then a bit faster, began to make my first mitt. Quite a few times I had to unravel the wool and start all over again, but Mama said that was how anybody learned.

As my mitt took shape, I found the pleasure of creating something. In a week, my first pair of mitts was finished, and I was delighted.

It wasn't until I put on the mitts that I realized one of them was quite a bit larger than the other. Mama laughed. "It might be a while before you're as good as Mr. Lonneberg, but these mitts will keep your hands warm."

I wore that first pair of mitts around the farm, pleased that I had made them myself.

After a few more cream cheques, Mama bought me another ball of wool so that I could make Arnfeld a pair of mitts. This time the two "hands" matched each other quite a bit better in size and texture. The mitts still weren't good enough for church or school, but they were just fine for farm use. I felt proud every time I saw them on my brother's hands.

Still, I always loved that first pair of mitts the most, and was very sorry when they wore out.

I also learned to make bread that winter, when Mama was laid up with a bad back.

Loading pigs to send to market should have been a safe, simple task. You just yelled a lot, and used a stick to persuade the pigs. But Mama loved to clown around, so she climbed a fence, grinning, to jump down at the pigs, waving her arms and shouting to scare them up the ramp into the wagon. At least that was the idea. Instead she landed awkwardly, collapsed on the ground, and shrieked with pain.

We carried Mama into the house and set her on the bed. She was in so much pain that she couldn't get out of bed for almost a week.

Bread had to be made every two or three days, so as the oldest kid, I was conscripted.

Mama kept the "yeast" growing in a jar in the pantry. Every week or so, she "fed" her yeast by stirring some potato water into the jar, and every few weeks she renewed the yeast by adding a dry yeast cake bought from Carl Christiansen's store.

Mama called instructions from her bed in the other room.

I started by "setting" the yeast that evening. "Heat a bit of water on the stove to lukewarm," called Mama. "Pour it into a cup. Add a few teaspoons of sugar. Pour in about half a cup of the yeast from the jar."

She continued. "Mix that together, and pour it into the big metal bowl. Add some white flour to make it kinda thick like stew. Stir it with a spoon. Gradually add about a quart of lukewarm water and stir it well."

"How much white flour?" I asked.

"About six cups or so," Mama said. "I don't know. Whatever it takes to make it kinda thick. Then wrap the bread bowl in the blanket real well to keep it warm until morning. That's it for tonight."

The next morning we carried on with our bread-making lesson. I was making heavy brown bread, using the coarse brown flour that Papa ground from our own wheat.

"Dump a bunch of the brown flour in the mixing bowl," Mama called from her bed. "Maybe about ten scoops full." The metal scoop was big. Mama always made ten loaves of bread at a time. "Mix in about a quart of lukewarm water."

"What do I mix it with?"

"The big wooden spoon. Then add more brown flour. And use your hands when the dough gets too heavy. Add more flour until it won't stick to your hands."

"How much flour?"

"I don't know. Until you can make it form a big ball in the bowl."

I added plenty more flour. "OK, I've got it into a ball."

"Sprinkle some flour on the kitchen table now. Put the ball of dough on the flour, and knead it. Push on it really hard, over and over again. Work the dough."

"The dough keeps moving away."

"You're not tall enough. Get the chair. Kneel on it."

"That works. I can hold it better that way."

"Knead it for about twenty minutes. Maybe half an hour."

My shoulders and arms were aching. Papa's coarsely ground wheat flour sure made for heavy dough. I hadn't realized that Mama was so strong.

"Now let the dough rise in the bowl. Wrap it again in the blanket. Put enough wood in the stove to keep the kitchen nice and warm."

The dough took almost two hours to rise. It smelled yeasty, and looked soft and spongy. I had to wake Mama up. "Now what?" I asked.

"Now punch it down."

The dough deflated, sagging as I punched it.

"Put a couple more sticks of wood in the fire to get the oven to stay at 350 degrees. Watch you don't get it too high. And you can start forming your loaves. Roll each one to get all of the air out."

By the time I got the loaves formed, the oven temperature had gone way down. Then I put too much wood in the stove. "Hey, the temperature is up to 450."

"Open the oven door," said Mama. "Fan the oven with a tea towel to cool it down. But don't let it get too cold. Rub the top of each loaf with butter. Then when the oven is ready, get them in right away."

Eventually I baked my ten loaves of bread, flipped them out on a rack, and let them cool. Proudly I stood gazing at those loaves. I had made them.

The fragrance of new bread filled the log cabin. I cut a crust, hot and steamy, spread butter on it, and tasted my first bread. Rich, dark brown, warm. Absolute heaven.

Better yet, that night, Papa ate three slices of my bread with his supper, three whole slices as he normally did with Mama's bread. "You did all right," he said. Absolute heaven, that, too.

ANOTHER SKUNK

"Archie! Archie!" Mama called through my crazy, mixed-up dream. There was so much noise, loud noise, shrill and shrieking, like hens in terrible distress.

Hens! I jumped up with a start. A light flared in the warm summer darkness. Mama was lighting the kerosene lamp, calling again frantically, "Archie! Archie! Get up!"

I leaped out of bed, pulled my clothes on, to the din of chickens squawking and screeching. Something was killing them. A coyote or skunk.

"Grab the gun," shouted Mama. She was heading out the door in her nightgown.

I grabbed the twenty-two, jammed some bullets in my pants pockets, and raced through the night to catch up to Mama.

How come this had to happen when Papa was away? Gone for a week. Out working for other farmers to get us some money.

Mama would expect me to do the shooting. As a thirteen-year-old, I'd been shooting cans and gophers and prairie chickens. But that was in daylight and without any pressure. This would be dark and chaos and screaming and feathers flying around.

The noise became unbearable as we reached the chicken coop. We smelled the problem before we saw it. Skunk. A thick, putrid smell.

I pointed the gun as Mama flung the door open, holding the lantern. Blood and feathers everywhere. Two chickens lay dead and torn. Our other chickens shrieked and squawked, flapping up and down and around, stirring the air frantically, hitting against each other and the walls of the chicken coop.

Then we saw it. A skunk crouched, back turned, tail up. Oh, no! The skunk pumped out a spray. My eyes misted over. I choked, gasping. The chickens flew around in even more panic, beating their wings in the air. I could hardly see the skunk.

Could I shoot that skunk? I lifted the gun. Chickens in front, chickens all around, moving, moving. My shot might kill them by accident.

The skunk scurried to one corner. There must be a hole there in the floor. The skunk was going to disappear. I had to get that critter right now, or it would be gone, only to return the moment we left.

I pulled the trigger. Deafening boom of the gun, my shoulder pushed back. Chickens flying around.

Overpowering smell now. Breathing almost impossible. There was the skunk, dead, blood, intestines. I'd hit the culprit. But in dying it had released all of the terrible oil in its scent gland.

Gagging from the nauseating odour, Mama and I looked in at the piece of black and white fur, the blood, and the guts. "Nice shot," gasped Mama, coughing.

I could hardly believe my good luck. I hadn't hit any of the chickens, not even one. Just the two dead victims of the skunk lay there. The rest of the chickens were flapping around, very upset, but very much alive.

"Let's get out of here," said Mama, coughing harder. "This mess can be cleaned up in the morning. Maybe some of the smell will die down by then."

Everybody was up when we got to the house, sitting around the kerosene lamp, eager to hear the story, gasping at the smell that permeated right into our log house and followed us on our clothes. Mama and I had to go outside again to leave our smelly clothes on the grass. Our clothes would have to be soaked in ammonia and scrubbed in carbolic soap.

After I crawled back into bed, I had a hard time getting to sleep again. Maybe it was the smell, or maybe it was the excitement over my lucky shot.

When I awoke the next morning, all was quiet except for birds chirping and singing in the trees. But the skunk smell was strong, even in the lean-to bedroom. I sure wasn't going to be the person to go back into the chicken coop and haul out that stinky skunk.

At breakfast, I asked, "So who is going to go into the chicken coop to get the skunk out?"

The silence was deafening. Everyone looked down. No one would meet my eyes, not even Mama. "Well, it sure won't be me," I said, trying to control my voice.

"Someone has to do it," said Mama quietly.

"Well, not me," I thundered.

"But, Archie," said Arnfeld, "*your* clothes are already stinky from the skunk."

"So you can wear them and go in there."

"Your clothes are way too big on me," said Arnfeld. "Your

pantlegs and sleeves would be way too long."

"You could roll them up."

"I could dig the hole for you to bury it in," said Arnfeld. "I'd dig it nice and deep."

We sat there in silence again. "It isn't fair," I said. "I'm the one who shot the stupid skunk." I stomped out, past my set of smelly clothes. The odour in the barnyard was unbearable. That skunk had to be buried, or the smell would never go away. But it was not going to be me going in to get that foul thing.

I tried to milk the cows, but could hardly breathe with the overwhelming smell of skunk. It would only get worse as the day warmed up. The skunk would start to rot. It had to be buried, the sooner, the better.

The only other logical person to do the deed was Mama. Her stinky nightgown was out there on the lawn, too. But it seemed ridiculous to imagine Mama in the middle of the day taking off all of her clothes and putting on her nightgown to go into the chicken coop.

Esther was only six. It didn't seem right to ask her to do it. Arnfeld was ten, a lot shorter than me. He could do it, but he would get his clothes smelly, too. That would mean one more set of clothes to soak in ammonia and to scrub with carbolic soap.

Sometimes skunk smell could be so bad you'd actually have to bury your clothes in the ground for a while to get rid of the odour. And sometimes the clothes would just have to be burned. I knew it didn't make sense to take a chance on wrecking another set of clothes.

I finished milking the cows, downright angry by now. It just didn't seem fair that I had to do the rotten job.

Everyone else was working so hard this morning, avoiding the issue, coughing, eyes running. The day was going to be a scorcher. The longer the skunk lay there, its guts decomposing, the worse the job would be.

By about eleven o'clock I went around the side of the barn. There was Arnfeld with the shovel, flinging dirt, digging a deep hole.

I sighed and stomped toward the house. There was Mama standing in front of our stinky clothes, almost as though she were ready to give in and put on her nightgown.

I sighed. "OK, you win."

Mama smiled, looking very grateful. "Thank you, Archie," she said, and left me to change into my smelly clothes from the night before.

As I reached the chicken coop, gagging, Arnfeld handed me the pitchfork. "Use this. You can keep the skunk farther away."

Then Mama appeared, looking sheepish, both hands behind her back. "I brought something for you." She lifted one arm forward, and there, in her hand, was a little bouquet of my favourite flowers: blue, purple, pink, and red sweet peas. What on earth was Mama doing with flowers at a time like this?

She brought the other hand forward and there was a piece of cotton string. "Tell you what," said Mama, grinning, "I'll tie this bunch of sweet peas over your nose before you go in there."

Sweet peas had the most wonderful fragrance, but this was really crazy. Still, what did I have to lose?

I shrugged my shoulders. "Well, I guess it can't hurt."

Mama wrapped the string around the sweet peas. I rolled my eyes as she stretched up to position the bouquet of sweet peas right over my nose, and tied the string around my head, knotting it behind my neck.

In I went, coughing, choking, eyes watering, pitchfork in hand. Thousands of flies were swarming around the dead skunk and the two dead chickens. Peering down through the soft blossoms, I stabbed the skunk's body, ran out, and dumped it into the hole that my brother had dug. Then back in I raced to get the two dead chickens and toss them into the hole, too.

Flowers tickling my nose, I grabbed the shovel and pushed dirt to fill the hole as quickly as possible.

I didn't admit it, but the wonderful fragrance of those sweet peas really did seem to help. Or was it the sound of Mama's gentle laughter?

MUGGINS

If Papa hadn't been hauling cream to Markerville, we never would have acquired our magnificent dog Muggins.

Papa hauled cream to earn money for our family. Dan Morkeberg made butter at his creamery in Markerville, but that was about ten miles from Dickson by terrible, rutty trails. It would have been foolish for each farmer to have to haul a gallon or so of cream each week to Markerville.

So farmers in our area brought their cream as far as Dickson, and from there, everybody's cream would be hauled once or twice a week to Markerville.

In the summer, farmers would chill their cream by hanging cans of it in water wells on their home farms. The day the cream was to be hauled, farmers would bring it to Dickson, setting the metal cans in a water tank to keep the cream cold. In the winter, cream cans would simply be left outside beside the general store until pickup by the cream hauler.

For years Papa was the cream hauler. In the winter our horses would pull the grain box, loaded with cream cans, on bobsled runners. In the summers, the grainbox, loaded with cream cans, rolled along on wagon wheels.

In the winter it was an especially long trip, at least four or five hours each way, with the team dragging the heavy bobsled through snow, maybe even through a blizzard. Papa would leave early in the morning, and he wouldn't return home until supper-time or later.

One frigid December morning in 1923, Mama heated stones in the oven of her cookstove—as usual—to keep Papa's feet warm under the blankets in the sleigh. Within a few hours the stones would have cooled off, but Papa would already be at Markerville.

The people at the Markerville creamery would fill an emptied cream can with steaming hot water to keep Papa's feet warm on the trip back home.

That evening, I'd been out milking cows, and was the first to greet Papa as he drove the team and bobsled into the yard. "Archie, guess what," said Papa. "I had something different to keep my feet warm on the way home tonight."

He lifted the blanket, and there, lying on his feet, was a huge pup with the biggest paws I'd ever seen on a dog.

The pup jumped down from the wagon and ran around me enthusiastically, his tail wagging.

"He's ours," said Papa, "from Dan Morkeberg."

I knew that Dan Morkeberg raised Saint Bernard dogs, but why would Papa be bringing one of them to our place? Dan Morkeberg's purebreds were expensive animals to be sold to city or town people.

"A pure Saint Bernard dog?" I asked, still puzzled, as the huge, furry pup cavorted about, with deep-toned yelping.

"Well, not quite," said Papa. "One of Morkeberg's best Saint Bernard dogs had puppies, but they were obviously not purebreds. Seems as though the dog had found herself some ordinary neighbourhood boyfriend. Anyway, Morkeberg is giving the puppies away. So I took the biggest one."

The door to the house opened. The rest of the family had heard the pup's happy yelping. They ran out, as excited as the puppy.

Before we went to bed that night we made a dog house of scrap boards, and gave the pup a big dish heaped with all of the warm leftovers from our supper. He wolfed the food down, then looked at us, tail wagging, as if to say, "Is that it?"

Back we went to the house. We filled the pan with bread, dumped in fresh, warm milk, and presented the mixture to the puppy. He gulped that down, too.

"The way he eats, this little muggins is going to do some pretty fast growing," said Mama.

"Muggins is a good name," we said.

Muggins loved to eat. Luckily we were on a farm so there was never a lack of food. The pup grew rapidly. It soon became apparent that he was going to take after the Saint Bernard side of his heritage.

By the time Muggins was a year old, he was gigantic, big enough to stand and look in the windows of our log house. He'd peer in the windows, calling us out, his deep, loud bark shaking the glass in the windows.

But Muggins was as gentle as he was large. At first we children were a bit afraid of playing with him because he was so overwhelming. We soon found out, however, that Muggins would never play rough. We could put our hands in his mouth, and he'd just close his mouth tenderly against our skin, hardly even letting us feel his teeth.

Mama could leave our baby sister, Alice, lying on a blanket out on the lawn, and Muggins would stand guard over her.

Muggins never would harm even the smallest baby chick. In fact, he protected our chicks and hens. Coyotes had become quite a problem with our chickens, sneaking into the yard when we were busy and committing murder.

After we adopted Muggins, we hardly ever lost chickens to the coyotes. Our hens and baby chicks roamed freely, protected by the gentle giant.

Muggins would chase coyotes from our yard, barking furiously, running after them, out into the field. A few coyotes tried to stand up to Muggins. The enormous dog would pounce, flashing his big teeth, sometimes drawing blood. The coyote would howl and race away. We'd laugh. "I bet *that* coyote won't be back." Muggins would even take on a whole pack of coyotes if he had to.

Muggins seemed to think that he should protect his humans from everything. If anyone drove a car into the yard, Muggins would bark at the car ferociously, as though this noisy creature meant us harm.

But to us children, and to the cats, the chickens, and all other little animals, Muggins showed the highest possible degree of gentleness. We all loved him and trusted him implicitly.

Then came the horrible November morning when Muggins appeared in the yard with a dead turkey in his mouth.

Sick in our hearts, we took the turkey from Muggins. Our neighbours, the Lonnebergs, raised turkeys. Any dog that would kill a neighbour's fowl would have to be shot immediately. There could be no second chance.

Raising fowl was an essential source of food and money for a pioneer family. No one could allow a dog to live if that dog was going to kill even one chicken or one turkey.

All of us, including Papa, looked sick. We could hardly talk. Papa went into the house to get the gun. As terrible as it would be, it would be better for Papa to shoot Muggins than to make Mr. Lonneberg do it.

We all knew that once a dog got the idea of killing fowl, that dog would do it again and again. You could beat the dog, even beat him in the face with the bird's blood-soaked body, but it wouldn't do any good. A dog that started killing fowl would always return to kill again. Our beloved Muggins would have to be shot, that's all there was to it.

We'd have to tell the Lonnebergs about their turkey, and it would be best to be able to say that we'd already shot the dog.

Muggins stood in front of us, blood and feathers stuck to his mouth, wagging his big tail, as though he thought he had done something good, as though he was trying to get us to praise him. Mama stood holding the dead turkey, silent, looking away.

I couldn't stand to stay around. I knew that everyone but Papa would go into the house as soon as Papa got the gun and tied Muggins up.

Heart aching, I headed out into the field, feet crunching through the layer of snow that covered the dirt. How I dreaded the sound of that gunshot.

As I walked, I realized that I was following Muggins's huge tracks in the snow. A spot of blood had dripped here and there beside his tracks. I almost turned off to go where there were no tracks, but something kept me following them.

All of a sudden I stopped. There was a terrible mess in the snow. Blood, lots of blood, and turkey feathers. And Muggins's big pawprints. But there were other tracks, too. Small pawprints. Coyote pawprints. With snow packed down all over, showing a scuffle, fighting, chunks of fur all over the snow.

There were two sets of coyote tracks, one set of tracks coming to the scuffle place, one set going away at an angle. Both sets of coyote tracks, coming and going, were spotted with blood.

I looked up and saw a coyote watching me from the edge of the forest. As I moved towards the coyote, it disappeared into the trees, limping, wounded, bleeding.

I started running. I ran as fast as I could towards home, yelling, "Stop, Papa, stop! Don't shoot Muggins! Stop, Papa!"

Faster I ran, until my lungs felt as if they would burst, shouting louder, hoping, praying that Papa would hear me in time.

Still there had been no gunshot.

Papa had heard me before I got to the yard. He stood there waiting, puzzled, gun in his hand. Muggins stood tied with a rope, tied short to a tree, his tail wagging.

The rest of the family had heard me yelling. They came out from the house. "He didn't do it," I said, gulping tears. "He was fighting off a coyote. Come and see. Muggins tried to save the turkey, that's why he brought it to us."

The whole family followed me out into the field. The story was all there in the snow: feathers and blood, with the coyote tracks, coming from the direction of the Lonneberg farm.

We stood there, trembling at what had almost happened. Then we realized that we'd left poor Muggins back in the yard, still tied short to the tree.

BERRIES AND BRANDING

Everything smelled so good one early August morning. Our whole family was up earlier than usual. No one had to be called twice. This was one of the most exciting adventures of the year. We were travelling ten miles by wagon to Kevisville, to spend the whole day picking wild cranberries and blueberries.

Even at a fast trot, it would take about two hours each way. That meant our team of horses had to get up earlier, too, so they could eat their breakfast of oats, and be brushed and harnessed in time.

Lunches had to be made. Sandwiches, lots of sandwiches, of fresh, homemade bread and butter filled with Mama's homemade cheeses, liverwurst, and dried beef. There were cookies, lots of them. For school, each person's lunch would have been stuffed into an emptied Roger's Golden Syrup pail or a lard pail, small metal pails with lids and handles, but today those smaller pails were needed for picking berries. Today, lunch for everyone was layered together into a big metal milk pail and covered with a tea towel.

Four-year-old Thora was excited about picking berries into her very own pail that Mama had given her. It was a Squirrel peanut butter pail with a full-coloured picture of a squirrel. Thora loved to keep things in that pail and carry them around. But today the peanut butter pail was empty, ready for the berries that she would pick all by herself.

We loaded the wagon with empty pails and empty cream cans. The pails were for picking berries, and when they were full, we'd dump the berries into the cream cans.

If we were lucky, we'd find lots of berries. The berries would be cooked with sugar—"canned" in glass jars for sauce, or made into jam. Hopefully we'd be able to get dozens and dozens of jars of berry sauce and jam, enough to supply us with wonderful eating for the whole winter.

We all rushed through breakfast, and Mama hurried to get

two-year-old Alice and our new baby brother, Walter, bathed and dressed. It was still chilly in the house. "Thora, you can wash yourself," said Mama.

Mama carried the metal wash basin full of hot water into the sitting-room/bedroom and put it right beside the new cast-iron McClary heater so that Thora could stay warm when she stripped to wash.

"Thora, hurry up," called Mama. "We're almost ready to go."

"Just my feet left," said Thora. She stepped into the pan, lost her balance, screaming, and fell with her back end against the heater.

Then there really was screaming, and crying. Everyone ran to see what had happened. There was the smell of burning cloth and burned skin. Thora cried and cried. The heater had burned right through her cotton underpants, burning deeply.

In the red, deep, awful burn in Thora's flesh, you could read a mirror image of the word "McClary." The raised metal letters on the heater had branded right into Thora's back end.

Poor Thora was shrieking with pain.

"She can't go," said Mama. "One of the bigger kids will have to stay home with her. She can't go picking berries today."

Thora shook her head, crying harder. "I want to go," we could hear between her cries.

"You can't go," said Papa. "Not with a burn like that. You can't sit in the rough old wagon for ten miles."

"I can stand up," said Thora, wailing louder.

"Don't be ridiculous," said Papa. "Maybe we should all stay home today. Thora can't stay alone and we need all of the bigger kids to pick lots of berries."

Mama nodded. "We can try again for a day next week."

Thora cried louder. "I can hold onto the back of the wagon seat and stand up."

We gave in and decided that because we were all ready, we might as well start out, and see how Thora got along.

Papa was driving the horses. Mama held Walter in her lap on the seat at the front. Her other five children sat on the wagon floor, between the cream cans, all except for Thora, of course.

Normally we took the trip at a fast trot, but today we travelled more slowly out of consideration for our burn victim. At first she whimpered with pain, but after an hour or so, she seemed to feel a lot better, and started to join in on the jokes and fun, still standing, of course.

We could hardly wait for the taste of the fresh blueberries. We knew where there would usually be great patches of berries.

This was the second most exciting day all summer. The absolute best was the Sunday School picnic, when each person would get an orange to eat, a genuine California orange, the only orange we received all year. We'd eat that orange, savouring each juicy section, trying to make it last as long as possible.

In a way, though, this berry-picking was almost better than the Sunday School picnic. You could eat as much as you wanted of the sweet blueberries, eat until you could hardly fit one more berry in your stomach, and still pick pails and pails full of berries to dump into the cream cans to bring home for canning.

Cranberries were too sour for eating (many) directly off the bushes, but we'd fill cream cans with cranberries, too, and bring them home for canning with sugar. They'd be delicious then, especially on chicken, pancakes, or pudding.

All the way in the wagon to Kevisville, I dreamed of berries, hoping we could fill all of the cream cans. Tomorrow the whole family would clean the berries. We'd roll berries, a few handfuls at a time, down boards that were covered with wool blankets. Leaves and twigs would adhere to the wool, and the berries would roll into a pan for washing.

Papa was a very fast berry picker, but we always teased him that his pails of berries were "dirtier"—littered with leaves and twigs— than those of anyone else.

It would take another whole day to process the berries, but at the end of it all, our pantry shelves would be loaded with glass jars of scrumptious jam and sauce. My mouth watered at the thought.

By the time we arrived at our berry patch, Thora seemed quite happy. Like the rest of us, she had to bend repeatedly all day, picking the berries from the ankle-height bushes, then standing up to dump the pailful into a metal cream can. We wondered how Thora would manage. But she seemed fine, picking into her little peanut butter can.

Most of us used Papa's homemade berry pickers, made by cutting a tin can in half and soldering a row of nails into one end. Using the nails as a comb, we tore berries from the bushes into the curved part of the tin can, ready to be dumped into a pail.

At lunchtime, we picnicked on blankets while Thora stood, happily chewing her sandwiches. We even kidded her about being branded with "McClary" for the rest of her life. She giggled with us.

Later that afternoon, when we'd found a fantastic berry patch, everyone was crouched down, picking through the thick bushes, when Thora started to cry.

"What's wrong?" asked Mama.

Thora wouldn't stop crying.

"Is your burn hurting?"

Thora shook her head, crying harder.

"Did a bee sting you?" I asked.

Thora shook her head again, crying more.

"Thora, tell us what's wrong," said Papa in a very stern tone of voice.

Thora wailed, "I lost the lid of my Squirrel peanut butter pail."

We had a hard time not laughing. We looked through the bushes, and Mama found the lid for Thora's pail.

We found so many bountiful berry patches that it was almost dark before we loaded the heavy cream cans up into the wagon and headed home. We might need two days to clean our generous harvest. We'd do the blueberries first because they were softer and more perishable. The cranberries could wait for a day or so.

I loved the sound of the hoofbeats and harness in the dark. Thora was still standing, holding on to the back of the wagon seat, nodding off, as though she would go to sleep. Everyone was quiet, feeling tired and peaceful. Every container in the wagon, even the picnic milk pail, was brimming with berries. Our faces and hands were purple and red with berry juice. Our stomachs were full and satisfied.

It had been a good day.

Chris and Christina Morck and their first two children, Archie and Arnfeld, 1913.

Dickson, Alberta, 1918, soon after the Morck family moved from Saskatchewan to live on a pioneer farm four miles from the town *(top)*. Esther at one year, with a new puppy, on the steps of the Morck's log house near Dickson, 1918 *(bottom)*.

The mischievous horse Little Queen loaded with Walter, Oscar, and Ella, and held by Thora. Bob, the dog, would help Thora chase Little Queen out of the slough every morning before school *(top)*. Ella Morck on Archie's horse Queenie. The horse on the right is Old Sock, 1932 *(bottom)*.

(Left to right) Arnfeld, Alice, Esther, Thora, and Archie Morck, circa 1934 *(top)*. The Morck farm with the new house, built in 1931. This photo was taken in 1935 *(bottom)*.

Neighbours help the Morcks saw trees into firewood for cooking and heating *(top)*. Papa (Chris) Morck (left) with a Danish hired man in front of a year's woodpile, circa 1935 *(bottom)*.

The Lutheran church in Dickson, Alberta, circa 1927.

A team of horses pulls out a stump, part of clearing the land in the early days.
Courtesy Glenbow Archives/NA-1691-3

The photo that was paid for by Mama Morck's chickens, 1939. (Left to right, back row) Thora, Esther, Alice, Walter. (Middle row) Arnfeld, Papa (Chris), Mama (Christina), Archie. (Front row) Ella, Paul, Oscar.

OLD SOCK

We kept a trustworthy team of bay-coloured work horses named Jack and Sock in the barn for everyday work: hauling manure or going to church, buying groceries in Dickson or delivering hay to the cows and the other horses. Both Jack and Old Sock were strong, willing, hard-working horses.

Sock was named for the band of white, like a sock, just above the hoof on one of her back legs.

She was a bit cranky, and we'd tease her, just to see her lay her ears back. Arnfeld, especially, liked to squeak "Sock! Sock!" in a high-pitched, taunting voice.

The more we teased Old Sock, the crankier she became. "Sock! Sock!" we squealed. She started to bare her teeth, which spurred us on even more. Old Sock become so annoyed that she'd reach towards us and snap her teeth as though she'd like to bite us.

Mama didn't like this at all. "Quit bothering that poor horse."

"But Mama," Arnfeld would reply, "when Old Sock gets mad, it's so much fun to watch."

"Well, she sure doesn't think it's fun," Mama always said.

As the months went by, as we continued to tease Old Sock, she would flatten her ears right back against her neck and snap her teeth so viciously that other people were quite scared of her. Arnfeld loved to watch this spectacle.

One afternoon, Arnfeld teased Sock as a group of neighbours, including a new Danish immigrant, visited in our barn.

One of the men, Pete Hansen, said to the young immigrant, "I'll give you twenty-five dollars if you'll stand right beside that Old Sock mare. I mean it, twenty-five dollars."

That was a lot of cash. But the young immigrant said, "Keep your money."

Mr. Hansen laughed. He knew his money was safe, because any stranger would be terrified to go near Sock. He didn't tell the Danish immigrant that Old Sock had never harmed anybody, and that the young man could have made easy money by taking up the bet. That horse had always been a pleasure to harness and work with, seemingly all bluff, no matter how hard we teased her.

When we'd drive the team to Dickson to get the mail and groceries at Carl Christiansen's general store, we'd tie Jack and Old Sock to the hitching rail. Old Sock had become so cranky that if anyone passed her on the wooden sidewalk, she would flatten her ears and bare her teeth. People would veer away, up against the store wall, or else approach the door from the other direction.

Arnfeld and I were working in the barn one day, and Arnfeld had been squealing "Sock! Sock!" as usual, almost crying with laughter every time the old mare reached out and snapped her teeth. Now Arnfeld was busy feeding the horses, forking hay into their manger.

But that afternoon, Old Sock had had enough. Just as Arnfeld put an armful of hay in front of her, Old Sock grabbed hold of Arnfeld's chest with her teeth, and lifted him up, right off the ground. "Help!" he screamed. "Help!"

Sock held Arnfeld up, dangling in the air, clamped tightly in her powerful teeth, then let him fall. Arnfeld hit the ground, rolling away, shaking. His shirt was torn, showing big teeth marks on the skin of his chest.

When Arnfeld had to show Mama his torn shirt and his wound, Mama said, "Too bad I wasn't there. It must have been so much fun to watch."

Old Sock never bothered Arnfeld again, but then, of course, Arnfeld didn't bother her again, either.

Roaring Twenties

My teenage years were the 1920s, the "Roaring Twenties." For our family the "Roaring Twenties" were indeed noisy—with the roars and wails of new babies, because during those years our family mushroomed. After our little sister Thora was born in 1920 (the same year that one-year-old Irene died), Mama had five more babies, all born at home.

Alice arrived in 1922, Walter in 1924, then Oscar in 1926. Our youngest sister, Ella, was born in 1928. In 1931, Mama gave birth to her tenth and final baby, Paul. With so many babies in our home, moments of silence were rare indeed.

I think the 1920s were actually called the "Roaring Twenties" because of all the new, noisy inventions. Cars roared through the muddy, rutty trails and usually became stuck, which made them roar all the harder. Young men on motorcycles began to haunt the countryside. Loud tractors took over the work on most farms, displacing quiet, faithful horses. Radios brought sound from miles away, right into your head.

Marconi's invention, the radio with earphones, had become *the* item to buy for your home. Radio owners were exclusive people who could talk about "the wonderful jazz last night from the west coast" and the "latest news broadcasts." Our family was very impressed.

I'll always remember the first time I listened to a radio. I was fourteen years old, so that would have been 1924. One Sunday at church our neighbours, the Westergaards, said, "Come to our place this afternoon and hear our radio."

Our dinner dishes were never washed as quickly as they were that afternoon, the horses were hitched back to the lumber wagon before they knew what hit them, and we all piled in and drove those two miles at a fast trot.

When we entered the house we saw Mr. Westergaard with a round object on each ear, a cord connecting them over his head, and that cord joined to a box. His hired man had a rig like that on his head, too, and it also was joined to the box. The two men seemed to be in a trance, but *we* couldn't hear anything. They looked up and waved happily at us.

Mrs. Westergaard said, "They're listening to a live broadcast from Calgary. That's a hundred miles away!"

We shook our heads in awe.

"We have only two sets of earphones," said Mrs. Westergaard, "so you'll have to take turns. We could separate each earphone set so four could listen at a time, but it's not as nice that way."

Papa said, "We'll take turns with the two sets as they are."

Mr. Westergaard handed his earphones to Papa. The hired man handed his to Mama. Our parents fitted the earphones over their heads, then took on that faraway look of wonder.

I decided that I might die if my turn didn't come pretty soon.

At last Papa took off his earphones and fitted them on Arnfeld's head, and Mama took hers off and handed them to me. Trembling with excitement, I put the earphones on. Like magic, from the very air around, I heard the song, "Oranges and Lemons."

The music was in my ears, clear and melodic, as if the singers were actually in that room. How could they possibly be one hundred miles away?

In a trance I listened, wishing that I could listen forever. "Oranges and lemons, say the bells of St. Clement's. You owe me five farthings, say the bells of St. Martin's."

A choir was singing right in my ears, a choir that was so far away. How could this be?

Papa tapped me on the shoulder when it was time for Esther and Thora to listen. I took off the earphones and returned to reality. The music was gone. But I could see it now in my sisters' smiles and in their faraway, unfocused eyes.

We each had several turns again that afternoon. But all too soon, hours had passed and it was time to go home to milk those blasted cows.

We didn't buy our own radio until 1937, and then for days we could hardly finish our chores.

Of course after having a radio ourselves for a while, we actually started taking it for granted. But never again could I hear that song "Oranges and Lemons" without feeling a shiver of delight and recalling that afternoon with the Westergaards, when I was fourteen years old and heard a choir from one hundred miles away.

PEANUT BRITTLE

One summer evening in 1925, Papa and Mama went out visiting and left the little kids at home in the care of Arnfeld and me. By then, Esther was eight, Thora was five, Alice was almost three, and Walter, one-and-a-half, just trying to talk.

That evening Arnfeld and I decided to do something special. Someone had given our family some peanuts, which was a treat. After we'd each eaten a few peanuts, Mama put away the rest so that we could enjoy a few more another time.

I decided to "stretch" the peanuts by making peanut brittle. Even with just a few nuts, we could make plenty of peanut brittle. Besides, it would be fun for the little kids and a good surprise for Mama and Papa.

We got out the largest of Mama's three recipe books. Sure enough, there was a big section on candies, including peanut brittle.

For two pounds of peanut brittle we needed two cups of peanuts. When we measured, we found that there was only one cup of peanuts. What did that matter? The candy would still taste fine with half as many peanuts per square inch.

Esther could read quite well, so we gave her the job of reading the recipe aloud. "In a large, heavy pan, bring to a boil one cup of water."

The biggest, definitely the heaviest, pan we owned was the cast-iron frying pan. Arnfeld dumped a cup of water into the frying pan and set it over the stove. I put more firewood into the firebox of Mama's cookstove.

The water soon boiled. "Remove from heat," read Esther. "Stir in, until dissolved, two cups of sugar. Then add and stir in one cup of syrup."

I measured out the sugar and the corn syrup, and Arnfeld stirred them in.

"Return to heat and cook to the hard-ball stage," read Esther. That made sense because we all knew that peanut brittle was supposed to be hard.

Arnfeld put the frying pan back on the stove, and I put more wood into the stove's firebox. The sugar dissolved, and the mixture started to bubble.

Even after the sugar mixture had bubbled for quite a while, it certainly wasn't forming a ball of any kind, let alone a hard ball.

We didn't know that candy stages, such as "hard ball," refer to the result when a spoonful of the hot sugar mixture is dropped into cold water, to show what the mixture will do as it *cools*.

If we had looked at the cookbook more carefully, at the very beginning of the candy section, we would have seen all of this. But we read only the page referring to peanut brittle.

Arnfeld kept stirring and I kept adding wood to the fire. The sugar mixture was still liquid.

"Esther, what does it say to do after it cooks to the hard-ball stage?" I asked.

"It says to add the two cups of peanuts and one teaspoon of salt."

"Well, it sure isn't hard, so I guess we can't add them."

"More fire, more fire," said Arnfeld.

"More fire, more fire," echoed Thora and Alice. Walter stood clapping.

I opened the firebox door and stuffed more wood into the stove. The kitchen was very hot. The mixture boiled and boiled and boiled. Arnfeld kept stirring and stirring. Still the mixture wouldn't harden, nor would it form a ball, as the recipe seemed to demand.

"Aw, just put in the peanuts and the salt," Arnfeld said.

So I did.

"What does the recipe say next?" asked Arnfeld.

Esther read. "Stir to submerge the nuts, and cook to hard-crack stage."

"Hard-crack!" I said, "We can't even get it hard. How are we ever going to get it to crack?"

"More fire, more fire," said Arnfeld.

"More fire, more fire," echoed Esther, Thora, and Alice.

I shoved in more sticks of wood. Sweat was running down our faces. The smell of hot sugar and burning wood almost choked us. The mixture boiled and boiled, the peanuts moving around as Arnfeld stirred. Still, the mixture would not turn hard.

Using the metal-coil lifter, I took off a large, circular lid of the stove top so that the frying pan could sit over the hole, in direct contact with the blazing fire below. But the mixture would not turn hard.

"More fire, more fire," called Arnfeld.

"More fire, more fire," echoed the little kids.

I put in more wood. The mixture had lost its sweet smell, was starting to turn dark, starting to smell burned. It didn't look the least bit hard.

"Esther, what does the recipe say next?" I asked.

"Well, after it cooks to the hard-crack stage, we're supposed to remove it from the heat and stir in two tablespoons of butter and a quarter-teaspoon of soda and one teaspoon of vanilla."

"Well, we can't remove it from the heat yet, because it sure isn't hard or cracking."

"More fire, more fire," called Arnfeld.

"More fire, more fire," came the echo.

The mixture boiled and boiled and boiled. It was getting thicker, more gooey, but it certainly wasn't hard like peanut brittle should be.

"What are we going to do if it never gets hard?" asked Thora.

"It will," said Arnfeld. "More fire, more fire."

To the echo of the little kids, I added more wood. I was starting to worry. This was definitely not looking or smelling like any peanut brittle that I'd ever seen.

"More fire, more fire," said Arnfeld. "We can't quit now."

"But it's turning black and it's smoking," I said.

Eventually we gave up. The mixture was a black, sticky, gooey tar.

Heartbroken, almost dizzy from the heat, we put the frying pan, with its gooey mixture, on the breadboard on the counter, then went to bed.

When we woke the next morning, Mama demanded to know what on earth was that rock-hard black stuff in the frying pan.

"Rock-hard?" we asked, in amazement. We ran to look at the pan. Sure enough, in cooling, the mixture had turned rock hard, crack-hard.

We told the whole story, expecting to be in trouble for wasting the peanuts, but Mama just laughed and laughed. "It's actually turned to charcoal now," she said. "Charcoal is supposed to be good for a laxative. Maybe we can keep it and use it. I can break pieces of it off to give to anyone who gets an upset stomach or needs a laxative."

And that's exactly what Mama did.

CHANGE AND CONFUSION

Whenever death came to a member of our community, everyone did what he or she could, through love and concern, just as had been done with my little sister Irene. No one would ever have dreamed of charging any money, not even one penny, for making a casket or preparing a body for the grave.

When I was a young teenager, some newcomers to our community lost a family member, and for some reason they *hired* the services of a mortician from Innisfail. It was quite a shock to the whole Dickson community.

The funeral was held in our church, and was run by the undertaker and his younger assistant. I was used to seeing only rough, bearded farmers and pastors, their complexions red-brown from sun and weather. These professionals had shaven faces and deathly pale skin. On their hands were grey silk gloves that reached above their wrists right into their blue-grey suits. Silk gloves on a man!

Flashing sleazy smiles, the two strangers ushered people into the church. Smiles at a funeral!

But most unbelievable of all, they were charging money for this.

I felt like shouting, "How dare you make money off a dead person." I said nothing, but I watched those two men in utter disgust.

Of course there are many extremely kind and caring people in the funeral profession, but my first introduction to the business was shocking indeed.

When I was growing up, many other confusing issues boggled my mind. One of the most puzzling was reproduction.

Sex seemed to be a sinful topic. If our parents caught us in curious play with certain parts of our bodies, we received a spanking and a harsh lecture. The neighbour children told us that doing "that" could give you an incurable disease, a punishment from God.

If these parts of our bodies and anything to do with them were evil, then how to explain the holiness of having children? Over and over again in church, we heard that marriage and children were precious gifts of God.

We often saw the mating of farm animals and the resulting drama of birth. It wasn't difficult to conclude that humans must also be created by similar mating. This jibed with the "sex education" we picked up from the neighbour kids.

Our parents never wanted to answer any questions about sex. They seemed ashamed of the whole business. Certain Bible passages seemed to confirm the sinfulness of sex, such as Psalm 51:5, where David said, "I was brought forth in iniquity, in sin did my mother conceive me."

If sex was evil, how could good Christian men and women, including my own mother and father, indulge in such activities?

In church I looked from one couple to another, trying not to think of them doing such a dirty thing. I counted their children. They must have been bad at least once for every child, so some couples must have been bad quite a few times. And my own parents . . .

Yet the Bible also said, "Be fruitful and multiply." Around and around my mind went, overwhelmed with the confusion.

As a young fellow, I also wondered why it should be so sinful for a woman to curl her hair with a curling iron heated over a lamp.

One Sunday afternoon a married couple, friends of my folks, visited us. The wife had just started using a curling iron the week before. Her husband and my father talked to her, discussing this as a serious sin. They said, "If the Lord had wanted you to have curly hair, He would have made you with naturally curly hair." The curly-haired woman and my own mother sat across the room, saying nothing, knitting ferociously.

Even worse was for a woman to cut her hair. During the early 1920s, church papers condemned this taboo in many articles, each proclaiming: "Bobbing hair is a dreadful sin. The Bible says a woman's hair is her crown of glory. Prostitutes in the red-light districts of the city started this evil practice of cutting their hair. Now ordinary women are doing the same thing and pretending to be Christians. What is this world coming to?"

Imagine the disgrace when many of the women in our own community cut their hair!

I thought the new short, curly styles looked cute, but I didn't dare to voice my opinion.

Even years later, when Esther at the age of twenty-one announced that she was planning to cut and curl her hair, Papa growled, "Then don't bother to come home, not ever again."

Esther did it anyway. When she dared to come home sporting her short, curly hair, Papa refused to speak a word to her during the entire visit. He just glowered.

When women finally won the right to cut and curl their hair and still call themselves Christians, they found themselves the target of more derogatory accusations. What now? They wanted to attend church without hats! Hadn't St. Paul written in the Bible that a woman must cover her head in church?

For years, women in our community who dared to come to church without hats were condemned soundly.

All that was nothing compared to a winter day when I was in my early teens and Arnfeld and I had stopped at Carl Christiansen's store for the mail. The annual meeting of the church congregation was in progress across the road, and we were just leaving the store to head home.

Suddenly we saw a man stride out the front door of the church, slam it shut, march in fury to the hitching rail, and grab his horse. Onto the animal he vaulted, and whipped it away, galloping down the snow-covered road.

Stunned, we realized that this furious man was none other than Carl Lorenzen, our good bachelor friend, always known to be calm and smiling. Carl never lost his temper. Impossible. And never would he whip a horse. Never.

We watched as Mr. Lorenzen whipped and whipped and whipped his horse, even though it was obviously galloping as fast as it could, until the horse and rider disappeared from sight.

When Papa came home from the church meeting we finally found out that Mr. Lorenzen had been nominated for the position of church deacon.

To everyone's astonishment, one of the old-timers objected. "In the Bible, St. Paul wrote that a deacon must be the husband of one wife, and Carl doesn't have a wife, so he can't be a deacon."

At first the other church members thought the man was joking, but no, he was adamant. Carl Lorenzen must not be a deacon. A hot debate broke out. "It just means that a deacon must not have *more* than one wife," said someone.

"No," said the old man, "it doesn't say anything about 'more than.' It just says a deacon must have one wife."

The old man convinced several others of his logic, and Carl Lorenzen had stormed out in anger.

In fact, Mr. Lorenzen was so disgusted that he cut off all his support of the Dickson congregation and joined the Kevisville church a few miles away.

People charging money for funerals, my parents hanging their heads at any mention of sex, good Christians fighting over Biblical interpretations—amidst all the confusion, as a teenager I knew one thing for certain: life had seemed a lot simpler when I was a child.

SMOKING

Then there was smoking.

On New Year's Eve, 1922, when our folks were out visiting, Arnfeld and I had stayed home to babysit. When Esther and Thora were asleep, Arnfeld and I decided to try smoking. What an exciting way to celebrate New Year's Eve! After all, I was twelve then, old enough to experience grown-up pastimes.

"Let's try Papa's fancy old pipe from Denmark," I suggested.

"It's broken. That's why he never uses it," said Arnfeld.

"That means he won't care if we use it. And it's just the bone stem broken off. We can wrap it with string."

I took the old pipe out of its splendid, velvet-lined case. "What can we use for tobacco? Papa must have taken it all with him."

Arnfeld looked around. "Cigar clippings."

We stuffed in the cigar clippings. I had to light about a dozen matches, nearly burning my fingers, trying to set fire to the clippings in the pipe, sucking hard on the stem as Papa always did. "OK, it's burning," I said at last, exhaling a puff of smoke, amazed at how terrible it tasted.

"Let me try," said my little brother.

We took turns, and were almost getting used to the awful taste, feeling very proud of our maturity, when Arnfeld became quiet and white.

"What's wrong, Arnfeld?" I said. "Talk to me. Are you all right? Oh, no!"

He made quite a mess all over the floor and in the chair.

After cleaning Arnfeld up and putting him to bed, I cleaned up the rest of the vomit, fighting hard to keep my own stomach under control. So our last few hours of that old year had ended on a sour note, and we were asleep before the new year arrived.

Still, I tried smoking again many times, often on the way home from school. The smoking rendezvous was a wooden culvert called Lund's bridge about half a mile south of Dickson. Several of us young guys would crawl into the culvert after school to practise smoking, feeling hidden from the rest of the world.

Some of the boys had older brothers who provided them with samples of tobacco. More often, though, we stole tobacco from our fathers. We used tissue paper when we didn't dare swipe cigarette papers from them.

I don't think any of us enjoyed the smoking, especially not at first, but it seemed that it was something that we were expected to do, and we were dumb enough to comply.

Lund's bridge culvert was wide enough and high enough to accommodate several young smokers. There we sat after school, smoking all we had managed to find each day, then proceeded on home, certain that our secret was safe—until one day when several of us boys were in Uncle Carl's store and some of the customers joked about "the culvert that smokes."

What a shock. We all stammered, red-faced, and left the store as soon as possible. It was several days before we met under Lund's bridge again. But the urge to be "grown-up" seemed irresistible.

Some afternoons, if we had no smokes to bring to our rendezvous, we'd go to a nearby spruce grove, tug some moss from the branches, and use this spruce moss as tobacco to roll cigarettes. It tasted awful.

Sometimes we'd pick withered rhubarb leaves and crush them for tobacco. Rhubarb leaves tasted *really* awful.

Once Arnfeld and I found a can that a tobacco chewer had used as a spittoon. It was completely full of thick, gooey, crusty spittle. It was hard to imagine anything less appealing, but we smoked that, too, rolling it in cigarette paper like regular tobacco. It was worse than horrible, but provided us with smokes for quite some time.

The older we became, the more the big boys shared their tobacco and cigarette papers with us, until soon we were rolling our own and smoking with them nearly every day.

When I was in grade seven, in early spring, one of the big boys brought a plug of chewing tobacco to school. By then I was one of the gang of "older boys" at school, and was therefore automatically included when the fellow passed out his chewing tobacco at noon. Each of us took a great bite of the chewing tobacco, and were expected to spend the lunch hour chewing and spitting.

Together we strolled to the slough between the school and Carl Christiansen's store, to a log raft we'd built especially for noon-hour sailing.

Standing at the edge of the slough, waiting for a turn on the raft,

I worked on my chew. It wasn't at all a pleasure, but what was a fellow to do?

"How's it going, Archie?" A classmate came from behind and gave me a playful but powerful nudge in my back with his shoulder. I almost landed in the water, but much worse, I swallowed the massive wad of tobacco. I gasped and stood up. It made a gruesome lump in my throat and stomach.

The raft came in. I took my turn, but felt relieved when the bell rang and we could run back for our afternoon classes. At least no one realized what had happened. For having swallowed such a big chunk of chewing tobacco, I wasn't feeling too badly.

But within an hour the classroom walls started to sway and the teacher's voice began to fade. I gulped. The walls wavered and my stomach started to heave.

I staggered to the back of the room and plopped myself on the bench behind the heater. The teacher stopped in the middle of a faraway sentence to come running after me. "Archie, what's wrong?" he asked.

I opened my mouth to answer, but quickly decided it was best to keep it tightly closed.

"Archie, please answer me."

I leaned on the ventilation pipe of the heater, wishing he'd send me home, but wondering how I could make it there. Maybe I could sleep right here by the heater.

Finally he gave up and questioned the others, but no one knew what was wrong with me. He continued the lesson, keeping his eyes on me. The rest of the afternoon passed in a swaying, sweating, shivering daze, with voices circling in and out of my consciousness.

After school Arnfeld pushed me up onto Old Bird to sit behind the saddle. He vaulted in front and we started home with me clinging to him. Bird seemed to understand my misery and refrained from her bucking trick.

At last we arrived home. Mama looked at my ashen face and trembling knees. "Archie, you foolish, foolish boy." That's all she said. She never asked what was wrong with me, even when she put me to bed. She must have smelled the tobacco on my breath.

One evening, I rode home from a school fair with a group of kids in the back of a big truck. Rain pelted down, beating on the canvas covering us.

"Archie, would you like to try a real cigarette?" said one of the boys.

"Where did you get it?"

"I bought a whole package. Real cigarettes. Look."

He gave me two. I smoked one right there in the back of the truck under the musty canvas. It tasted better than all of the other strange things we'd been smoking, but it still tasted pretty bad. What worried me, though, was that smoking was starting to feel like a pleasure, like filling some kind of emptiness or need.

The next day I was out in the woods fixing a fence and felt an overwhelming craving for the other cigarette in my pocket. I sat on a rock and lit up. Sitting there puffing, I thought, "This smoking is trapping me. I don't want a stupid habit to control me."

So I decided to give up smoking. Believe it or not, I was already hooked badly. For days, no, for weeks, I fought the powerful craving to smoke. That really scared me, that something could have such a strong grip on me.

I vowed that I never would start again, because I realized that the longer I smoked, the harder it would be to quit the next time. But I did give in. For another few weeks I smoked again, hating myself. After an even harder struggle, I finally quit, and I was still only fourteen years old.

MAMA

Mama worked incredibly hard to care for her many children. Being poor created a lot of extra work.

For school, each of us boys had only one pair of pants and one shirt. Each girl had one school dress. That was it. The minute we arrived home we had to change into our old work clothes.

Still, the school clothes often became soiled, and usually at least one child's school outfit needed to be washed at night so that it could be worn the next day.

We had no washing machine until 1927. That first "machine" was just a round wooden tub with no motor, which was operated by pushing a lever (attached to gears) back and forth, back and forth.

Before that, all of our clothes had to be scrubbed out by hand. Our faithful mother worked late every night scrubbing and rinsing clothes, then ironing them dry so that each of her children would find a school outfit hanging by the kitchen stove, ready for the day ahead.

We each had one pair of shoes. On Saturday nights Mama and we older children scraped off the week's accumulation of mud and manure, washed each person's shoes, let them dry by the stove, then applied a liberal coating of black shoe polish and "elbow grease" until all of the shoes shimmered for Sunday morning church service.

During all of the years that we were growing up, Mama sewed most of the clothes for our family, using the sewing machine that she had brought with her in 1909 on the ship from Denmark. That machine was powered by rocking the treadle with her foot, hour after hour.

It was impossible those years for Mama to keep up with all the work. Sometimes the house would be untidy, the babies would be dirty and screaming, a button might be missing from a shirt (even though Mama had been sewing and patching until the wee hours the night before), or the meals might not be ready on time.

Papa could not understand such things.

Sometimes, when Papa impatiently criticized Mama's house-keeping, she would look him straight in the eye and retort with a strong voice and a wry smile, "Chris Morck, you couldn't cook or keep a house if your life depended on it. If I hadn't married you, you would have starved to death years ago."

Sometimes when the work was all done, Papa played with us, but Mama was our real companion. She could turn nearly any task into fun. Before we knew it, any job could be done, and done well, without too much pain, thanks to Mama and her antics.

Mama loved to clown. Digging and picking up thousands of potatoes to store for winter hardly sounds like fun, yet because of her, it was tremendous fun.

Mama was just over five feet tall. Papa was over six feet tall. Dressed in Papa's overalls, many sizes too big for her tiny bones, our mother kicked up her heels and jumped around, turning our huge garden into a stage for a comedy.

"Look out," Mama might call, as she tossed a squashy, rotten, frozen potato at one of us when we bent over. Then again, she might not warn us, either.

She'd croon and prance, or make exaggerated huffs and puffs, as she carried pails of potatoes, until we'd roll around on the ground laughing.

During cold nights, none of us, especially not the little children, would want to dash through the snow to the outhouse. So during the night we'd do our business indoors, in a white enamel-coated metal chamber pot.

One morning I happened to be in the yard when Mama was carrying out the big chamber pot, swishing with the night's collection of urine, ready to be dumped into the outhouse. Just at that moment someone walked from our tree-lined lane into the yard.

Mama assumed the person was Arnfeld or me, and headed straight for him, swinging that full pot around and around like a lariat, calling, "Yahoo! Yahoo!" with centrifugal force keeping the liquid inside the pail.

The person stopped abruptly. Suddenly Mama realized that

this young man was not one of her sons, but a young neighbour named John Nissen.

Probably Mama was embarrassed, but she certainly took it as a good joke on herself. She gave the chamber pot one more swing, and said, "Hi there, John. Nice to see you."

John Nissen mumbled something, his face much redder than Mama's.

Winter Work and Snow
Pudding

Every winter evening we stoked up the fire in the cast-iron heater in the sitting-room/bedroom. We hoped to persuade a bit of heat to travel through the doorway into the lean-to bedrooms. The lean-to had absolutely no insulation, so we who inhabited it needed plenty of quilts at night. Sometimes we even wore toques to bed.

No matter how much we built up the fire before we went to bed, it would be so cold in those two bedrooms that, in the light of the lantern, we could see our breath as though we were smoking.

No matter how much wood we dared to put in the heater before going to sleep, the fire always burned out during the night. The entire log house would be freezing cold by morning.

Arnfeld and I tried to be the first ones up every morning to start the fire in the heater and in Mama's cookstove so that the other members of our family wouldn't have to get up to a cold house.

Every night we laid out wood, kindling, and matches, all ready for the morning, piled beside the stove in the kitchen and beside the heater in the room where our parents and the youngest babies slept.

Arnfeld and I woke early and lay shivering for a few minutes, gathering courage to leave the wool quilts. Finally, in our long underwear, we would make a dash for the heater, shovel the cold ashes out into the ash pail, stuff in the wood, arrange the kindling, strike a match, then stand shaking with cold until the fire spread its glowing warmth.

Mama and Papa always greeted us from their bed. Mama smiled and thanked us every morning. Her smile alone could warm a room, and made getting up to start the fire completely worthwhile.

After we lit a fire in the heater, Arnfeld and I always went out to the kitchen to clean out the ashes and start the fire in the cookstove. There we stood in our long underwear, warming up some more, dressing by the warmth of the fire.

Next, we raided the cookie jar and headed outside to do our chores before breakfast.

After breakfast, there was always time for family devotions, no matter how many chores remained. Papa read from the Bible and prayed, then we all joined in with the Lord's Prayer. Immediately after we said "Amen," Papa would always say, "Hitch up, boys," expecting us to leap up and get busy with our work.

We joked that we were quite old before we realized that the Lord's Prayer didn't end with "Amen—Hitch up, boys."

To me, Papa's phrase came to symbolize a good approach to life. You didn't just pray and sit around waiting for things to happen. You prayed about something, and then you got busy and worked your best with it, too.

One winter morning, my parents had a harsh disagreement, and Papa stomped out right after breakfast without conducting devotions. That morning, while he was cutting trees for firewood, the axe glanced off the tree and sliced his ankle very badly, laying him up for weeks.

Mama insisted that it happened because they had been angry and unforgiving and hadn't started the day with devotions.

Every Saturday during those winters, Arnfeld and I helped Papa chop trees for firewood, then pile them high above our heads in a rack on the bobsled runners. Poor Old Sock and Jack sure had to work to haul those loads of logs home.

By the time I was about fourteen and Arnfeld about twelve, we could do this job by ourselves on Saturdays, working all day long as soon as the snow was deep enough for the bobsled. Arnfeld and I would be doing well, though, to bring in three loads of trees each Saturday—one after our morning chores, and two in the afternoon before evening chores.

By the beginning of February, each farm had a mountain of tree-length logs ready for sawing. All the farmers of the community worked together, spending about two days at each farm.

One man owned the saw, a circular blade powered by a putt-putt engine that was extremely difficult to start. When the man finally revved up his little engine, the day's work would proceed. The owner of the saw usually operated it—few people would want that dangerous job.

Four or five men wrestled with each log, feeding it into the saw, which sang a deafening, shrill song as it sliced through the wood.

There were hundreds and hundreds of trees to saw, to be wrestled with hour after hour. Another man, standing on the other side of the saw, grabbed each heavy slice as it dropped from the blade, and flung the sliced blocks into piles.

By the beginning of March, each farm in the Dickson community had its mountain of logs transformed into a mountain of blocks, ready for chopping.

The wood split properly only when frozen hard as glass. Arnfeld and I worked long hours to chop that wood as soon as possible, splitting a whole year's supply within a month or two, before spring came. If left to thaw in April, the wood became tough and soggy, very difficult to split.

Even when it was frozen solid, splitting wood was an exhausting job. But I didn't mind it, not when Arnfeld and I worked together. We passed the hours telling crazy jokes in exaggerated Danish accents, puffing and panting as the piles of split wood mounted.

Every February, when the farmers came to saw our logs, they always teased Arnfeld about the snow pudding. Mama was famous in the community for her delicious snow pudding, a light, fluffy, white dessert made of egg whites, cornstarch, sugar, and vanilla, which would be topped with preserved cranberries or blueberries.

Mama didn't make snow pudding very often because it took a lot of time and energy to hand-whip the egg whites. All of us, including the six or seven farmers who came to our farm to saw our logs, always looked forward to the treat of snow pudding.

Arnfeld had been just a little guy when he was given the job of watching the snow pudding, after Mama had cooked it, because it had to sit outside to cool. "Arnfeld, you just sit right there and watch the pudding," Mama had said. "Don't let the dog or any other animal touch it."

When Mama had entrusted the big bowl of snow pudding to Arnfeld's care, she had left a wooden spoon in the pudding. "Stir it once in a while," she said, "so it cools nice and smooth." Then she went back into the house to finish preparing a scrumptious dinner for all of us, especially for the volunteer sawing crew.

At last dinner was ready. Mama sent Arnfeld to summon the work crew, and without noticing anything unusual, brought the snow pudding in for dessert.

The dinner was delicious. But everyone was looking forward to the snow pudding. Mama passed the dessert bowls and spoons around, then set the bowl of snow pudding on the centre of the table.

The guests were told to help themselves. I watched the first of the farmers dip in the big wooden spoon, expecting to scoop up a nice, rounded serving of pudding, fluffy and spongy, like white chiffon. His joyful expression changed to surprise and disappointment as the spoon came up with just a watery liquid.

"What on earth?" said Mama.

She grabbed the bowl and peered into the pudding, lifting it, pure liquid, with the spoon. "What happened?"

She turned to Arnfeld. "Why is it so runny? Did the dog get into this? What happened?"

"No," said Arnfeld adamantly, "no animals got into it, honest. I watched it all the time."

"Well, something happened," said Mama. "It wouldn't just turn all watery like this. Did you do anything to it?"

Arnfeld turned red and looked down.

"Arnfeld," said Papa, angry. "What did you do?"

Arnfeld said, "Well, I just tasted it."

"You had no right to do that," said Papa.

"What else did you do?" asked Mama.

Arnfeld's lip was trembling. "Well, I tasted it a few times, and then quite a bit of it was gone, so there might not be enough. I needed to make more, so I just stirred in a few big handfuls of snow. Well, it's called snow pudding."

Papa's face was furious, but the rest of Arnfeld's explanation was drowned out by the laughter of our guests. They laughed and laughed. "Snow pudding. So he added snow. Oh, that's a good one. Snow pudding. He added snow." They slapped their thighs, laughing harder and harder.

Papa's scowl soon turned to laughter, too.

Years later, whenever the farmers gathered to saw wood at our place, they always asked Arnfeld, "So are you going to help your mama with the snow pudding this year?"

PNEUMONIA

Arnfeld and I made rafts with logs for the sloughs around the farm. In the spring of 1925, when Arnfeld was twelve, we had an early thaw, so we had perfect rafting conditions.

When the Westergaard family came to visit on a Sunday afternoon, we went rafting with their three boys. It was a cool afternoon with a brisk wind. Still, the temperature was above freezing and the sloughs were liquid.

Arnfeld lost his balance, fell off the raft, and soaked his clothes, but he was having much too much fun to go in to change into dry clothes. He just kept playing, rafting, and shivering for an hour or two.

When we came home, Mama wasn't pleased to see her soaking son tremble uncontrollably. The Westergaards went home, and Arnfeld was put to bed under a couple of quilts.

By morning Arnfeld was one very sick boy, coughing and feverish with pneumonia.

Mama made mustard plasters for Arnfeld's chest. To make a mustard plaster you mix about a tablespoon of mustard with three tablespoons of flour and enough water to make a paste. When these three things are mixed, they react together to make heat. The heat of mustard plasters was about all that the early pioneers had for treating chest infections, including pneumonia. There were no antibiotics in those days.

Mama mixed mustard plasters every few hours, spreading the warm paste on cotton cloths and layering them over Arnfeld's feverish chest. A mustard plaster has to be watched carefully or it can become too hot and burn—a fresh one should be applied for no more than about ten minutes. And the skin must be rubbed with baby oil first.

Mama tended to Arnfeld through each day and each night. We took turns looking after him, but even then she hardly slept. Arnfeld became more and more sick, and we were terrified that he might die.

We all did a lot of praying.

There was talk that maybe Arnfeld should be taken into the Innisfail hospital. But the weather had turned cold again and the roads were impassable. Another woman in our community had pneumonia. Her family had tried to take her into Innisfail, with a team of horses pulling her in a sleigh, over those twenty-five miles of awful trails in bone-chilling weather. The sleigh had tipped, she had fallen out into the snow, become even sicker from the cold and exposure, and died.

Mama was not going to let anyone try to take Arnfeld out to travel for hours in the snow and freezing cold. She knew that a doctor couldn't do much for pneumonia, anyway, just keep a patient quiet and warm, and that's what she was doing. And Mama was praying.

Arnfeld lay day after day, burning with fever, hardly responding when we spoke to him, weak, as though he really were not going to make it. Mama became more and more exhausted as the days and nights wore on. "He's going to get over it," she kept saying. "He is. God will take care of him."

On the tenth day, Arnfeld's fever broke. He sat up and started to talk. "Where am I? What's going on?" We hovered around him, excited, trying to answer his questions, jabbering, all of us at once, all except Mama. I looked around for her. Mama had gone over to sit on a chair, hands together on her lap, face uplifted. "Thank you," I heard her murmur, "thank you, thank you."

Then Mama went into the kitchen to get Arnfeld something to eat. And over the next few days, she nursed her young son back to health.

The Concrete House

Our neighbours, the Lonnebergs, had a terrible fire in their wooden house one night when I was in my early teens. It was caused by a Little Wonder heater, the kind of airtight heater that Mr. Lonneberg had warned us about the night when we first moved to Dickson.

I remember seeing the flames blaze through the night sky, all the way from our place. I remember running, running through the snow with Mama and Papa and some of the kids to try to help the Lonnebergs. The rest of it was just like a bad dream of flame and heat and crying.

The Lonnebergs' house was destroyed, but luckily none of their family was hurt.

Although Mr. Lonneberg was a carpenter, when he built a new house, he used neither logs nor lumber. He decided to build the new house of concrete. This proved to be a brilliant idea. Not only was it more fire-safe, but it also couldn't harbour bedbugs, the curse of pioneers in our area.

In 1926 the Lonnebergs moved to British Columbia. Our family knew that we were going to miss them terribly, but we were thrilled about renting their quarter-section of farmland and their three-bedroom concrete house.

There were seven children in our family by then, including Oscar, who had just been born that fall. We'd been feeling a bit crowded—to say the least—in our log house, even with the two extra bedrooms in the lean-to. How unbelievable that we would be able to live in a real three-bedroom house with a large living room and kitchen!

How unbelievable, also, that we wouldn't have to deal with bedbugs.

On moving day we found one more bonus: a cat. The Lonnebergs' cat was still there in their yard. We'd always admired that cat with his eyes of two colours, one blue and one yellow. When we found him, his tail was half frozen off, but he was still as friendly and gentle as ever. We named him S.P. Lonneberg, and he became part of our family.

We loved the Lonnebergs' place, but two unfortunate events happened on our first Christmas Eve there . . .

As always, after Christmas Eve supper, we joined hands and danced around the Christmas tree, singing our favourite carols, eyes sparkling with the light of the white candles on the tree.

Mama had sewed new matching dresses for six-year-old Thora and four-year-old Alice. The dresses were made of orange and yellow flowered material, with scalloped, cream-coloured collars. Of course both sisters wore their fancy matching dresses for such a special occasion as Christmas Eve.

Singing and dancing around the Christmas tree, Thora twirled and pranced, proud of the full, round skirt of her new dress.

Suddenly, Mama was hitting Thora, spanking her on the bum again and again. "Thora! Thora!" Mama was yelling. Thora started to cry. Why would Mama suddenly be hitting Thora? Soon we realized that the back of Thora's skirt had caught fire from a Christmas tree candle, and Mama was trying to beat out the flames.

Papa grabbed the blanket off their bed and wrapped Thora in it, suffocating the flames. But what was left of Thora's dress certainly didn't match Alice's dress any more.

On that same night, our beloved dog, Muggins, wagged his tail and woofed his enormous bark when Mr. Lorenzen arrived to share our Christmas Eve supper. Of course, with all of the other Christmas Eve celebrations and with Thora's dress on fire, no one had been outside watching Muggins, but when anyone had used the outdoor toilet that evening, Muggins had followed along, romping in the snow.

Just before I went to bed, almost midnight, I decided to pay a visit to our outhouse. There, in the open entry way to the house, Muggins lay quietly. Thinking nothing, I went to the outhouse. When I came back, I bent to pat Muggins. He didn't wag his tail or move at all.

"Muggins," I called. He still didn't move. I pushed him up, but he just flopped back down.

"Help!" I yelled. "Something's wrong with Muggins."

Muggins was dead. He must have suffered something like a heart attack or twisted bowel.

In shock we knelt beside Muggins, talking about all the chickens he'd protected, how he had watched over us, the fun we'd had playing with him, how he'd tried to rescue the Lonnebergs' turkey from the coyotes, the surprise when Papa brought him home as a puppy. Shivering from cold, we hugged his huge, furry body, reluctant to leave him out there on the porch, so we kept talking in the frigid air. Finally we had to go into the house, where we stood shaking around the heater, trying to warm up the ice-cold feeling inside. We had lost a good friend. It was a Christmas Eve we couldn't easily forget.

PASTOR NYHOLM

Most pioneer children finished their schooling at the end of grade eight. In those days hardly any farm parents saw the point of more education for their family. Children represented cheap and essential farm labour.

In the 1920s, our nearest high school was twenty-five miles away at Innisfail. It was bad enough to think of finding money for school books. What farm family could pay for a child's room and board in Innisfail?

A very few parents scraped up enough money so their daughter could become a teacher or a nurse, or so their son could become a teacher or even a doctor. But those parents were the rarest of exceptions.

There was absolutely no chance that *our* family could find money for room and board for me. Besides, Papa needed me on the farm.

Grade eight ended with province-wide departmental exams. Our local teacher would never be allowed to preside over such important exams, so a member of the school board would supervise us. He solemnly read the long list of rules, opened the sealed envelope, handed out the papers, then strode up and down the aisles, his shoes squeaking, as we wrote frantically, our hands and wrists aching, our throats dry with tension.

I did quite well on those exams, and received a treasured diploma. But that meant my school career had ended.

My last day of grade eight, the end of June 1926, was one of the most terrible days of my life. Behind Arnfeld, I rode home depressed and despondent. Further schooling for me seemed impossible. I was nearly sixteen years old, and I felt that the future held no hope for me. I would have cried if Arnfeld hadn't been there.

Over and over again, all the way home, in time to the rhythm of Old Bird's plodding steps, I heard these terrible words in my head: "I'm finished. I'm finished. I'm finished."

Thank goodness for an American man named Pastor Nyholm.

In 1929 our church at Dickson brought in a new pastor. He was Paul Nyholm, a young man who had been teaching at Dana College in Blair, Nebraska. Because Pastor Nyholm had been suffering from nervous tension, his doctor had told him to quit teaching and move to a rural parish. In those days, Dickson, Alberta, was about as rural as you could get.

Pastor Nyholm and his new bride had lived only in big American cities. They had always had electricity, running water, and indoor plumbing. Of course there were no such things in Dickson. We were all worried about how the Nyholms would fit in.

The church council members decided to buy the Nyholms a special welcome present, an expensive, new Coleman lamp that used pressurized gas.

The members of the church council tried out the new Coleman lamp before the Nyholms arrived, to be sure that it worked perfectly. Everyone was impressed. It gave off much more light than our kerosene lamps, and didn't act ornery like Aladdin lamps.

Papa and some of the other church council members gathered at the parsonage on the evening of July 3rd, 1929, to be there to welcome the Nyholms when they arrived. I went along, too.

We all stood around, excited and nervous, as the Nyholms drove into the parsonage yard in their big, black Essex car.

Smiling broadly, the tall, slim pastor introduced us to his vivacious wife, Ingfrid. Pastor Nyholm looked dignified and handsome. They were both immaculately dressed, but also so friendly that we soon felt at ease in our old, worn farm clothes.

When we were showing the Nyholms around the parsonage, Mrs. Nyholm said, "I don't even know how to light a cookstove or a heater." She laughed, a soft melodic laugh, her eyes shining. "I bet you all find that hard to believe."

"I don't know how to light them, either," said Pastor Nyholm. "You're sure going to think we're dumb."

Papa said, "I'll be glad to show you." And he did. They listened carefully, and soon understood.

It was starting to grow dark. One of the farmers held up the new Coleman lamp. "This will have to do instead of electric lights. We hope you don't mind too much."

"Of course not," said Mrs. Nyholm. "We hope you don't mind showing us how to use it."

"Well, first thing, a Coleman lamp can be very dangerous if you aren't careful. It uses high-test gasoline." He showed the Nyholms how to operate the tiny pump to pressurize the gas in the little tank at the base. "The gas burns in these two mantles."

Mrs. Nyholm reached her hand towards the two tiny gauze bags that were the mantles.

"No!" everybody shouted. She pulled her hand away, looking startled.

"You can't touch the mantles if they've ever been lit before," Papa explained. "They'll crumble into ashes."

We showed the Nyholms how to light the mantles, then adjust the valve to make the mantles glow with a brilliant white light. The gas burned with a soft, steady hiss. To us, this Coleman lamp was a marvelous new invention, and for the Nyholms it was primitive and old-fashioned.

We all looked at Pastor and Mrs. Nyholm, hoping for their approval. "It gives off a beautiful light," said Mrs. Nyholm, smiling broadly.

As they had done for all their pastors, the farmers brought firewood, and then families gathered to split a year's supply of wood for the cookstove and heater in the parsonage. Pastor Nyholm watched us splitting wood and asked, "May I try?"

"Of course," someone said, handing him an axe.

Pastor Nyholm took a mighty swing at the block of wood—and missed. With a determined expression, he swung again—and missed.

We looked at one another. Even very young boys and girls were expected to be able to handle an axe. And this was a grown man!

Pastor Nyholm swung again. Not even close. A child giggled, and soon all of us were laughing. How shameful to laugh at a pastor, but we just couldn't help it.

Pastor Nyholm swung again. This time the axe glanced off the wood, but the next time he missed again. He looked up at the ashamed, laughing faces circled around him. "Just you wait. I'll learn." And he started laughing, too.

How we loved him, from that moment on.

Pastor Nyholm had a special interest in young people. It really bothered him that there was no high school in our area. Repeatedly he spoke to the church council about starting a high school. "If nobody else can do anything about this situation, then the church must."

A world-wide economic depression was starting to take hold just then. This hardly seemed to be the time to launch new ventures, especially one so overwhelming as starting a high school. But under Pastor Nyholm's ceaseless prodding, some members of our congregation formed a Dickson High School Association. They received approval and a grant from the Department of Education, but the new high school still had to charge forty dollars a year tuition per pupil.

In September 1930, four years after I'd had to quit school at grade eight, the new high school opened in the basement of our church in Dickson. Elsa Gundesen (one of my primary school teachers) was chosen to be principal. Pastor Nyholm would teach some of the classes.

One of the young women in our community, Margarethe Nissen, enrolled as both a student and a teacher. The Nissens were immigrants from South Denmark, which had been under German rule. Fully fluent in German, Margarethe taught that language.

The church basement was full of big wooden desks built by local farmers, who had charged nothing for their labour of love. There was no shortage of students to fill those desks. Students came eagerly—young people from our community and from neighbouring areas, plus some recent Danish immigrants.

Arrangements were made for girls from other districts to stay with farm families. It was assumed that boys were hardy and could find their own accommodations. A few boys stayed in the Gundesen farm home with the principal and her widowed mother, but others just fixed up abandoned shacks around the area.

"Papa, can I go to the new high school?" I asked, my heart pounding. "Even just one year. Just grade nine?" I was now twenty. Surely I had a right to go to school if I wanted.

"Archie, we can not spare you from the farm," said my father. "You know we can't do without you here. And where do you think you would get money for tuition and books?"

So I looked on from the sidelines when the new school started. But at least now there was a high school in Dickson, only four miles away, within a dream's reach, thanks to Pastor Nyholm.

POOR PRICES

Because Alberta is one of Canada's prairie provinces, you could still call me a "prairie" boy, even though I lived in Alberta's west-central woodlands. But there has always been a tremendous difference in climate between Alberta's dry, windy southern grasslands (what we called the real prairie) and our rainy, green woodlands.

During the whole decade of the 1930s, the skies above southern Alberta seemed to have forgotten how to rain, yet in our area west of Innisfail we always had enough rain.

People who lived on the real prairies in the 1930s called the depression years "the Dirty Thirties" because powerful winds whipped the powder-dry topsoil through the air, mile after mile, until you could hardly ever see any horizon. Blowing topsoil filled the ditches level with the roads, and even piled up high enough to bury fenceposts.

Choking and coughing became a way of life for the people who lived in the dust-bowl, as their summer skies churned with thick, black, stinging dust.

We, in Alberta's woodland area, were so much luckier. We had rain and little wind. We could always grow good crops. Our only problem was that, because of the economic depression, we could scarcely get any money for what we produced.

From 1929 on, the price of farm products plummeted further every year. I remember one Sunday afternoon visit, when the discussion turned—as usual—to the financial situation.

"Who'd ever believe," said my father, "that all you get nowadays for a two-hundred-pound hog is three dollars? And a nice, fat steer brings about eighteen dollars! That's an insult for all the feed and care that goes into raising an animal."

"Did you hear what Carl Lorenzen is doing?" one of our guests asked. "He's giving cattle away!"

"Giving them away?"

"Yeah, he's decided to help feed poor families by giving them each a steer as a present, to butcher. He says he feels a lot better doing that than selling cattle for eighteen dollars."

"I know how he feels," said a neighbour. "I quit selling my eggs. Why should I sell a dozen eggs for eight cents? I just give them away, too. And if none of my neighbours can use any more, I break the extra eggs into the horses' oats."

"Yeah," snorted another neighbour. "Eight cents for a dozen eggs ain't worth the wear and tear on the poor chicken's private parts!"

Everyone roared with laughter.

One of the men leaned forward and almost whispered. "I hear the jobless people in Calgary are planning a rebellion."

"Aw, that'll never amount to anything. They're too busy trying to find something to eat."

"Good thing the government set up bread lines and soup kitchens, or the city people would be out here mobbing us for food," said one of the men.

"Well," snorted Papa, "the government had to do something. It's all their fault, this blasted depression."

"At least the western provinces have outlawed foreclosures. Think of how many people would have lost their farms otherwise. It's more than Bennett with the federal government ever did for anybody. I'm ashamed to think that such a lousy prime minister is an Albertan."

And on it went. Every time people gathered, they complained.

Our family sold cream, so that usually provided us with enough cash for salt, coffee, and sugar.

One afternoon I walked into the house, smelling something scorched. "Mama, what's burning?"

She chuckled. "There wasn't enough money for coffee this week, so I'm trying to make some by roasting wheat kernels in the oven."

When I tried to drink the wheat brew, my face wrinkled. It was awful stuff. "Well," I said, "at least it'll cut down on the time we waste having coffee breaks."

Every year of the depression was worse than the one before it. We were all so short of money. Even the farmers who had been giving away their cattle and eggs became desperate enough to take whatever price they could get for their produce.

Then one day, a neighbour came into Carl Christiansen's store for his mail. "Oh, good," he said, "this must be the cheque from the cattle I shipped to market last week. I sure need it. Me and my family are just plumb out of money."

"Bet that cheque will hardly be worth cashing," said one of the farmers, "the way the price of cattle has been falling."

"Yeah, you might get a couple of dollars per steer, or something ridiculous like that," said another.

"Anything is better than nothing," said the man, opening the envelope. His smile vanished, to be replaced by a look of horror. "I don't believe it. This can't be true."

"What's wrong?" We all rushed over to him.

"A bill! They say *I* owe *them* money."

"For what?"

"For freight." He looked ill. "They say it cost more for the railway freight charges to ship my cattle than what they sold for at the market! Where am I going to get the money to pay this bill?"

In the weeks to come, many more farmers had the same horrible experience, having to pay a bill when they sold cattle.

Soon no farmer dared to send livestock away to sell. What family could take that chance?

TO KEEP GOING

No matter how scarce cash became during the Great Depression, our family of nine children still needed the occasional new clothes. With rough farm work, our clothes wore into tatters and shreds. Mama sewed as much as possible, but still it took money to buy fabric for sewing.

The cheapest way to buy fabric and clothes was by mail-order catalogue. Every few months we'd write up an order after spending evenings diligently studying the "Farmer's Bible" (the T. Eaton & Co. catalogue).

Mama would sit by the kitchen table, filling in the long order blank. "Archie, you need overalls. Thora, you must have material for a dress. Papa, you need socks and overalls. Walter and Esther have to have shoes."

"Mama," we'd say, "you need material for a new slip and a dress."

Mama would place her own most essential items at the bottom of the list, then add up what this was all going to cost. Inevitably the sum would be too great. You can guess whose essentials were dropped from the list.

Mama would sew herself a slip from the white cotton sacks that our flour had come in. Never mind that the flour came from our local store so the sacks had big letters in indelible black ink stretching like a beauty-contest banner diagonally across her bosom and tummy, proclaiming, "CARL CHRISTIANSEN & SONS."

"Well, at least we're not at war," Mama would say. "Compared to the jobless in the city, we live like kings. And think of all the poor farmers on the prairie. At least we have rain so we have food. We can eat as much as we want of eggs, cream, milk, meat, our own cheese, bread from our own wheat, porridge, potatoes, vegetables . . . "

"Yeah," we'd tease her, "the only reason we can eat as much as we want is because they're not worth anything."

In those depression days, we could not have grown any crops without having horses. Horses asked only for water, grass, hay, and maybe a pail of oats now and then. Never did horses demand things that had to be purchased: gasoline, oil, or expensive spare parts.

No car, truck, or tractor could need so little and produce so much—even fertilizer! You could not run a vehicle without money. You could run a horse without having one cent.

Vehicles couldn't reproduce themselves. Horses could! They were real heroes.

In the years before the depression, many farmers had bought tractors, trucks, and cars, but in the 1930s no one could afford to run them.

Horse-drawn buggies and wagons were dug out from the junk heaps and put back into active service. When the old wagons wore out, no one had money to buy new ones. So people dismantled their once-treasured cars down to the wheels, axles, and frame, and attached a wagon-tongue so a team of horses could pull what was once an automobile. They fit a wooden box on top to give a comfortable wagon, ready to be pulled by a team of horses to transport grain, wood, or whatever.

Some people left their car's top intact and added shafts to make a fancy covered buggy for one horse to pull to church, to town, or even to school with a load of kids.

Our family just kept repairing our rickety old wagon with scrap boards.

Our old school horse Bird served faithfully, her steel-grey coat turning white with the years. As more children were born into our family, Old Bird took them to school, bucking them off gently whenever it pleased her, waiting patiently for them to remount so she could take them safely home.

On the weekends, Old Bird worked hard in the fields. And sometimes Papa would even let her into the barn when he was milking cows.

One spring when Arnfeld and I were grown young men, farming with our father, Papa said, "Old Bird shouldn't have to work in harness any more. If she can just take the little kids to school once in a while, that's enough."

So that Saturday, when Papa hooked up horses for ploughing, he left Old Bird in the pasture. Papa hadn't been ploughing for more than a few minutes when he heard pounding hoofbeats and anxious whinnying.

Old Bird! She had jumped the fence.

She galloped to Papa, lined herself up with the other horses and pretended to plough, too, her hooves digging into the heavy earth, her neck arched, her muscles straining. All around the field, Bird plodded beside the team.

Finally Papa had to give in, unhook one of the other horses, and let Old Bird work.

LITTLE QUEEN

When Old Bird was really too old, Papa bought a small horse that Esther and Thora could ride to school. My sisters called her Little Queen. She was brown with a black mane and tail, bay-coloured, a very pretty horse.

But Little Queen didn't always want to take Esther and Thora to school. She plodded on the way to school and sped up for the trip home. The girls soon learned that they had to leave plenty early to get to school on time.

One morning Little Queen decided that she would carry Esther and Thora only as far as the top of a certain hill. The hill happened to rise from the edge of the Lonnebergs' land that we were renting. When Little Queen reached the top of the hill, she turned around and headed back home, totally ignoring the two little girls kicking her, yelling at her, pulling hard on her reins.

When Little Queen reached the yard, Esther, who was in front, turned the horse around, and made her go out of the yard again. But again, the horse went only as far as the crest of that hill, turned around, and headed home, oblivious of any efforts to the contrary.

Once more they tried, desperate, knowing that by now they'd be quite late for school. Little Queen reached the crest of the hill the third time, and again headed back home with Esther and Thora crying in frustration.

I decided I'd better do something about this stubborn little animal. When the girls came back into the yard, I asked them to get off their horse. "I'll show her," I said, picking a willow switch.

When Little Queen took me to the top of the hill, as before, she stopped and turned towards home, ignoring my reining. But when I hit her with the willow switch, she soon changed her mind and decided to go in the direction of the school.

"Let's try that again," I said to the little horse. I turned her back towards home. She walked fast and happily in that direction. I turned her around, headed to the hill again. She walked slower and slower and came to a stop at the crest of the hill. Again I hit her with the willow stick. Again, she decided it would be best to go over the hill and keep heading towards school.

"Let's do that once more," I said, turning her back to try the hill again. This time, with a loose rein, Little Queen just continued in the desired direction.

I turned Little Queen back home. Esther and Thora got on her, and I walked beside them to the hill. Little Queen kept going over the hill and carried her young passengers to school. Of course they arrived very late, but at least they did arrive.

Little Queen was a smart horse. She never did the hill trick again.

Instead, she'd go partway to school and then just lie down. The two little girls would kick and yell and hit her, but Little Queen would just lie there. Whenever the horse decided to get up, Esther and Thora would climb back on, and often end up late for school again.

In the mornings Esther usually made the school lunches for herself and Thora, while Thora went out to catch Little Queen and get her saddled and bridled, ready for their journey.

Little Queen's pasture had a deep slough full of water. One morning, when Thora was chasing Little Queen around the pasture, trying to catch her, the horse waded into the middle of the slough to escape being caught.

Thora stood there, frustrated, knowing that she and Esther would be late for school again.

But Thora outsmarted Little Queen that time. She went back to the yard to get our new dog, Bob. "Sic 'em, Bob," said Thora. Bob ran through the cold water to bark and nip at Little Queen's heels.

The horse finally gave in, walked out of the water, and allowed herself to be caught, but Esther and Thora were late for school again.

Little Queen seemed to enjoy replaying this trick of standing in the water. Thora got into the habit of automatically taking Bob along every morning to chase the horse out of the slough.

When Alice started school, Papa made a little buggy and a pretty red sleigh so Little Queen could pull the three girls to school, regardless of the weather.

One cold winter day, Esther, Thora, and Alice hooked Little Queen to the sleigh. They arrived at school late. Because they had trotted the horse, her long winter coat had sweated up—soaking wet.

They didn't have a blanket along because they had expected, as always, to put their horse in the school barn. More than the normal number of kids must have ridden there that morning, because the school barn was full of horses.

There was absolutely no room inside the barn for Little Queen. Her wet hair was steaming in the cold air, and the girls could find no blanket or anything to put over their horse, but they were already late, so they tied Little Queen to a fence and went into the schoolhouse.

Back at the farm the next day, Little Queen was running a fever. She had contracted pneumonia.

Through the nights, Thora and Alice insisted on taking turns with Little Queen in the barn. Arnfeld and I took turns, too. None of us slept much.

"Little Queen, you might have done some bad things, but you sure didn't deserve this," said Esther. "We love you, we really do."

"Even if you were kinda naughty sometimes," said Thora. "We really do love you."

We made compresses by stirring hot water into a bag of grain to keep Little Queen warm under her blankets. Nothing seemed to help. The horse became more ill by the hour.

"We love you, Little Queen. Please get better," said Esther, her arms hugging the horse's neck, but the animal just lay on the straw, weak, listless, unresponsive.

"We're sorry," cried Thora. "Please get better. We are really sorry that we left you outside when you were sweated up. We are really sorry. Please get better."

"Yeah," said Esther, "it was all our fault. We are really sorry."

By the fourth evening, Little Queen was dead.

LEFT OUT

Before the Great Depression hit, Papa bought two more uncleared quarter-sections. In the summer of 1930, some young Danish immigrants, unable to find work elsewhere, helped clear and break our new land in exchange for room and board in the concrete Lonneberg house that we were renting. But there was talk of the Lonnebergs returning from British Columbia, and there was no way that our parents, we nine children, plus four or five boarders could move back into our two-room log house with its little two-bedroom lean-to.

The Morck family had to have a new house. The Danish immigrants agreed to help us build a two-storey house on our new land. Again they would work for free, in exchange for room and board, which was fine because there was plenty of extra food around—we couldn't sell farm produce for anything anyway.

For lumber, we'd use wood from trees that we'd cleared from the land. We'd haul wagonloads of trees to the sawmill in Raven. They would saw our logs into boards, taking some of the lumber instead of money for our payment.

There would be very little expense in building the new house. We'd need nails, windows, and doorknobs, but we could trade produce for such things at Carl Christiansen's general store.

The main thing we needed was labour, and the strong, eager immigrants provided it.

The new house was to have four bedrooms upstairs and one bedroom downstairs. It seemed too good to be true.

Our house was also to have real plaster on the inside walls and on the ceilings, so there would be no bedbugs! Just thinking about moving back into the old log house was enough to make us scratch.

While Alice, nearly eight, looked after little Oscar and Ella, our (again pregnant) mother, with the help of thirteen-year-old Esther and ten-year-old Thora, had to cook meals and bake bread for all of our family and the boarders, too. Feeding at least fifteen people every meal, week after week, proved to be quite a task.

Mama had always made cheese for us, but now she was making extra cheese to sell at Carl Christiansen's store. She made cheddar and white caraway, stacking them on racks, rubbing them every day with vinegar so they wouldn't mould. The cheeses sold well, but didn't bring much money, and it seemed as though there was never enough money to buy even the everyday things for our whole family.

A month after the new Dickson High School was opened, in October 1930, Papa came back from taking a load of wheat to Innisfail. "Archie, it's a good thing we didn't waste money on tuition and books for you to go to school," he said. "Thirty cents a bushel. That's what I got paid today for the wheat. Last year at this time we got $1.30 a bushel."

"Maybe next year I could go to school, start grade nine." I spoke quickly, trying to get the words out before Papa could argue. "I'll be twenty-one then, and maybe the grain prices will be better."

"Maybe they'll be worse." He glared at me. "Thirty cents a bushel can't pay any expenses for growing the grain, let alone buy school books for a dreamer. I don't know how we'll even survive if things get any worse."

So I worked for another year, clearing land, cutting trees for our new house and for firewood, splitting wood, working on the new house, growing crops, tending livestock, watching my friends go to school.

In March 1931, Mama's last baby, Paul, was born. Now there seemed to be even more work to be done, extra water to haul and heat for washing diapers, more firewood to heat that water, and so on.

I wondered if I dared, but one evening in early August 1931, my desperation gave me the courage to bring up the subject again. While we were eating supper, I asked, "Papa, when can I ever go to high school?"

"This fall," he snapped.

I almost dropped my fork.

"But only for one year," Papa said. "Only grade nine. We'll let you try it. As long as you keep up with all of your farm chores every day, before and after school."

I was so happy I couldn't speak, just sat there with a silly grin on my face.

"But first, Archie, we have to finish building our house, get everything moved to the new house and the new farmyard, finish the haying, and harvest all of the grain. School starts September 1st, but *you* won't be starting then. We might not be finished harvesting until the end of October, you know."

"Yes, Papa," I murmured, so happy that I hardly knew what to say. "Thank you."

We worked frantically on our new house that summer, whenever the weather didn't allow haying.

By the middle of August the house was almost finished. Mama said, "Let's try to be in our new house on Archie's birthday." My birthday was August 25th. That sounded like a good idea. The sooner the better so I could get to school without being too many days or weeks late.

Completely unknown to me, my parents had invited the whole neighbourhood for a combination surprise birthday party and house-warming party, set for the evening of my twenty-first birthday.

All that day of my birthday we worked, trying to finish moving everything to the new house and farmyard by suppertime. It was hard work because the new place was almost a mile away from where we were living at S.P. Lonneberg's concrete house.

It was a long day and everyone was hungry. We were going to have supper in our new house that night. Mama came out to the yard at about six o'clock and said, "Supper is almost ready. Unharness the horses. We've done enough for today. Clean up and change your clothes. This is a special celebration. Archie's birthday and the first meal in our new house! You guys go shave. You look so scruffy."

"Let's just wash and eat," I said. "We have to leave the horses harnessed. We can do some more moving after supper. At least we should get the chickens moved tonight."

"We can move them tomorrow," said Mama.

"No." I tried not to yell. "We have to move them tonight. Maybe we can do some haying tomorrow. I want to get haying and harvesting done so I can get to school, you know, before Christmas."

No one paid any attention to my arguments. Everyone got dressed up for supper. My brothers shaved. I sat in my dirty overalls, several days' growth of beard on my sour face, and fumed through the meal. Putting the last forkful of food into my mouth, I stood up. "Come on. Let's go get the chickens tonight."

No one made a move.

"It's my birthday. You'd think someone would want to help me, to cooperate with me on my birthday. OK, never mind, you lazy things. I'll do it by myself." I stomped out of the house.

I was flinging the harness back on the horses when one of our neighbour families drove up, dressed in their best clothes.

Then I realized what was happening. Grinning broadly, my heart pounding with excitement, I ran full speed for the house to wash, shave, and change my clothes, but before I reached the house, another two neighbours (dressed in their best) had driven into the yard and caught me in my dirty, dishevelled state.

Within minutes our new yard was full of horses and wagons and people and laughter.

It was a great party!

We did get the chickens moved and the haying finished. Harvesting went well, but it was early October before we shovelled the last load of grain into the granary and Papa announced, "Archie, you can start school tomorrow if you want."

So at the age of twenty-one I began grade nine, and loved it, even though I had a month's work to catch up on. How good it felt to be learning again, no matter how long and tiring the days might be.

That school year went so fast. When I finished grade nine in the spring, my father said, "That's it. I can't spare you any more from the farm." So I had to quit school again.

My nineteen-year-old brother, Arnfeld, was desperate for schooling, too. Our next brother, Walter, was only eight, Oscar was six, and Paul was one, so it would be ages before they'd be grown up enough to take over the heavy farm work. But maybe we could take turns at schooling, Arnfeld and I.

One day Arnfeld brought up the idea. "Papa, Archie is of age. And I soon will be. We have a right to an education. What if Archie and I took turns, one of us working on the farm and the other going to school?"

Papa exploded. "This depression is killing us and you think we should find money for sending you to school. I don't want to hear another word about this school business."

Our bachelor friend, Carl Lorenzen, loved horses and owned quite a few. My favourite was a friendly, beautiful buckskin mare called Queenie (no connection to my sisters' Little Queen). One day when I was patting Queenie, Mr. Lorenzen said, "Archie, I want you to have that horse."

I argued half-heartedly, but he insisted. I could hardly believe it. A horse of my very own.

We used Queenie in the fields, but whenever I got a chance I'd ride her. She was so fast. Galloping on her brought tears to my eyes. Just having Queenie helped get my mind off school for a while, helped ease the frustration and impatience I was beginning to feel at home.

Already twenty-two years old, I couldn't see how I could ever afford to get my high school education, let alone university and seminary. Both Arnfeld and I dreamed of being missionaries or pastors, but that seemed impossible.

That fall, an evangelist suggested that we older boys who were having trouble finishing our schooling could take a shortcut into the ministry by becoming evangelists. All we really needed, he said, was a bit of Bible school training.

I was thrilled with the idea. But when I talked to Pastor Nyholm about my new plan, he said, "No, Archie. Get all of your schooling somehow—high school, university, and seminary. There's nothing like a full education to prevent somebody from going off half-cocked and making a fool of himself and of religion."

But how could I ever find enough money to finish school?

THORA'S CAKE

One Sunday afternoon in August 1932, an older couple, who had no car or horses, walked a mile to our place for a visit. We decided that it would be fun to take them for a Sunday drive to see all the beautiful crops in the neighbourhood. I hooked Jack and Old Sock to our wagon. Mama, Papa, the visiting couple, Arnfeld, Esther, and I all climbed into the wagon.

Thora was staying home to look after the little kids. "Thora," said Mama, "I don't have a cake for coffee. Could you make one for when we get back?"

"Sure," said Thora. She was about twelve at the time.

As soon as Mama and Papa left, Thora fired up the cookstove, mixed the ingredients for a white cake, and when the oven temperature reached 350 degrees, poured the batter into a fancy, fluted pan to bake. This pan would make a tall, impressive cake.

For a while Thora stayed in the kitchen, tending to the temperature of the oven, adding more wood carefully to the firebox of the cookstove to keep the temperature as close to 350 as possible.

But it was such a beautiful day outside. Ten-year-old Alice, eight-year-old Walter, six-year-old Oscar, four-year-old Ella, and even one-year-old Paul were all outside having a good time playing. Thora decided to go out and play with them.

Thora stuffed quite a bit of wood into the stove. She knew it would make the temperature go up a bit high, but it would keep the cake baking for some time without more wood. Out she went to play for a little while.

A little while turned into quite a while because the kids started playing baseball, and Thora wanted to play with them. The ball game was so much fun. When Thora finally remembered the cake, she ran into the house.

The oven temperature was just right, about 350 degrees, and the cake was golden brown.

Thora took out the cake and turned it upside down to cool. But the cake broke open. It was raw and gooey in the middle. The oven must have been too hot, causing the cake to bake too quickly on the outside so that the inside didn't have a chance to finish cooking.

Quickly Thora flipped the half-raw cake back into the pan, but it broke some more, almost in half, and now looked awful. Thora shoved it into the oven again to finish baking, and immediately started mixing up the ingredients for another cake.

As soon as the broken-up cake was baked right through, Thora turned it out onto the table, washed the pan clean, and put the second cake into the oven to bake, carefully adding wood to keep the oven at the correct temperature.

The second cake turned out to be perfect.

But what could Thora do with the first cake? It looked like a disaster. Mama and Papa must not see it, or they would know that she had wasted ingredients because of her carelessness the first time.

The evidence had to be disposed of. It was unthinkable to throw food away. Thora called all of the kids in. "Come eat some cake right now."

Alice, Walter, Oscar, Ella, and Paul all came immediately. Thora gave them great big pieces of the first cake. It looked funny, but it tasted pretty good. The kids ate and ate until the cake was all gone.

"Now, don't you dare tell Mama and Papa that I gave you this cake," said Thora. "No matter what. Don't you dare tell them that you had any cake to eat already."

When we all returned, and sat down together for "coffee," Mama praised Thora for her beautiful cake.

Mama served a piece of the lovely dessert to each adult and each child. But of course the children were so full from the first cake that they could hardly eat another bite.

"Are you not feeling well?" Mama asked her little children.

"No, we feel fine," they said.

Mama felt their foreheads. No fevers anywhere. Everyone looked healthy.

Mama shook her head, totally puzzled. She never did figure out their mysterious loss of appetite.

DEPRESSING POLITICS

The principal of Crescent Heights High School in Calgary, William Aberhart, was the first and last man to interest me in party politics. He captured the interest of thousands of other frustrated Albertans, too.

William Aberhart set up a Calgary Bible school called the Prophetic Bible Institute, which flourished in the early 1930s. Despite the economic hardships, radio had become the great medium of mass communication.

On Sunday afternoons Aberhart conducted an hour-long religious broadcast. Almost every Sunday afternoon our family would just happen to find ourselves visiting any of our neighbours who happened to have a radio.

As the months went by, more and more people in our community and in all of Alberta were listening to Aberhart's church service.

At first Aberhart's Sunday broadcasts involved merely the expected evangelistic sermons and hymns. Then, on one of his broadcasts, Aberhart revealed that an English economist, Major C.H. Douglas, had proposed a political system called Social Credit to give the common people a share in all of the profits of a country. The depression was hitting harder and harder. Who wouldn't be interested in hearing about such a system?

Soon Aberhart's Prophetic Bible Institute broadcasts dealt more with the Social Credit philosophy than with religion. We were told that every citizen had the right to a reasonable profit from all industries. The profits of financial powers were created by the labour of common people who received no share of the wealth.

This share, Aberhart's persuasive radio voice assured us, must be returned to the people who did the sweating and the toiling. Large corporations should be forced to return their profits, in the form of monthly dividends, to every worker and producer in the society.

Then one Sunday, Aberhart announced that every adult Albertan should be entitled to about twenty-five dollars a month as a fair share.

Twenty-five dollars a month! The popularity of Aberhart's broadcasts soared.

He used Biblical prophesies to substantiate his new political theories as God's way of bringing fairness and equality to everyone. From radio speakers across the province, our prophet's voice boomed, slamming governments, both federal and provincial. Without reserve, Aberhart accused all of the government leaders and their "henchmen" of being crooked, evil, and responsible for all of our problems.

After a few weeks of government slandering, Aberhart announced that God had called him to form (and to lead) a Social Credit party. With our support, this party would win the impending provincial election, and after that important first step, would begin to lead the whole country to righteousness.

If Christians in Alberta would rally to the cause, Aberhart told us, the other provinces would eventually follow. Hopefully the time would come when Canada would be governed totally, provincially and federally, by a Social Credit system.

There just happened to be an Alberta provincial election coming up in September 1935. Aberhart promised that if we elected him and his party, each Albertan would receive a twenty-five-dollar monthly dividend. We fell for it, hook, line, and sinker.

For the first and last time in my life, I became an ardent party politician.

Over the next few months, every Albertan house blessed with a radio was packed on Sunday afternoons as friends and neighbours sat on chairs, boxes, and the floor to hear the answer to our economic woes.

Schoolhouses and community halls all over the province became the scene of packed, fervent Social Credit meetings.

Alberta resounded with Aberhart's theme song, the Christian hymn "Oh, God, Our Help in Ages Past." We sang it with gusto at each meeting, we heard it over the radio, we hummed it as we did our farm chores.

Once a week, people crammed into the schoolhouse in Dickson for our community's Social Credit meeting. Anyone daring to question the Social Credit speakers would be looked down on as foolish or immoral. To our dismay, our own church's beloved Pastor Nyholm questioned everything to do with Social Credit.

At one meeting, Pastor Nyholm stood up and asked, "Where is the money going to come from to give every Albertan twenty-five dollars a month? The whole economy, including the business and industrial community, is bankrupt from this depression. Hundreds of businesses have already closed down, and the rest are operating on shoestring budgets. So where is this money going to come from?"

That night a young schoolteacher stood to scorn Pastor Nyholm. "Imagine, you, a so-called educated man, unable to understand a simple concept that we have explained carefully, over and over again.

"Or, Pastor Nyholm," his voice thickened with sarcasm, "is it that you don't *want* to understand? You call yourself a pastor, eh? And yet you ridicule the only possible solution to your people's financial problems? For shame!"

We listened, and although we dared not jeer at Pastor Nyholm, we glared at him with such disdain that he realized we supported every word of the young man's tirade. The room was silent. Pastor Nyholm looked from one face to another, then sat down in horrified and pained submission.

A few days later when Pastor Nyholm came to our place for a visit, I told him, "You should be happy. I'm going to use my twenty-five-dollar monthly dividend to continue my schooling. You are always telling me I must continue my schooling, even when Papa says there's no money."

Pastor Nyholm shook his head sadly. "Archie, you'll never see one cent of that dividend, not ever."

Infuriated by the assurance with which Pastor Nyholm denounced my dreams, I began to feel very bitter towards him.

One other person, an old schoolteacher whom we called "Uncle Chris," also refused to support Social Credit. Together, the American pastor whom we had respected so much, and the teacher whom we had known and loved for years, dared to stand against our fervour. We ostracized them and ignored their obvious pain.

Albertans wanted to believe that any change had to be for the better. When the election came in 1935, the polls were swamped. Social Credit won by a landslide, taking fifty-six out of sixty-three seats. Liberals, Conservatives, and United Farmers of Alberta members lost the seats they had held for years.

William Aberhart became premier of Alberta, with Ernest C. Manning as secretary. A whole new slate of cabinet ministers appeared, everyone totally inexperienced, yet zealous to Social Credit.

What a relief! This was the first Social Credit government in the world. Alberta would be a model to the world. Now, at last, the domination of financial powers had been broken—at least in Alberta. Now, at last, we could claim our fair share of the profits of the economy. Now, at last, we would receive our deserved twenty-five dollars every month.

Pastor Nyholm was right. We never received one cent.

To our anguish, Parliament ruled the Social Credit proposals as *ultra vires*, that is, beyond the powers of a province as outlined by the British North America Act.

Many Albertans contemplated rebellion, suggesting that Alberta become an independent country so it could follow the Social Credit doctrine. But nothing happened.

Aberhart laid total blame at the doorstep of the parliament buildings in Ottawa. So the only hope would be for Social Credit to gain political control of Canada, province by province.

Meanwhile, the new government had to settle down and administer the province of Alberta. It was to be the best and the most honest government ever in power, for hadn't we all sung "Oh, God, Our Help in Ages Past"? And hadn't Aberhart assured us that God was on his side? At least Christian men were in office. They weren't greedy for money, power, or personal gain. How naive we were.

The new government produced a "prosperity certificate," roughly resembling a dollar bill. This was also called "scrip" and was designed to circulate more money.

To bypass the constitutional prohibition against a province creating its own currency, the Social Credit government required the scrip-holder to affix a one-cent stamp on the back of the bill each Thursday.

At the end of two years there would be $1.04 in stamps, so you would have spent more than a real dollar if you held on to the scrip. But if you kept it for a week, you would have paid only one-cent rent for the use of a whole dollar. And if you spent the scrip before Thursday, you would have had the use of a dollar for nothing.

So pass scrip on, spend it, and create prosperity. It seemed like a good idea at first.

Storekeepers such as Carl Christiansen, who supported Social Credit, would accept this "funny money" and would give it in change. But no one was obliged to accept scrip. Many stores, especially those in the cities, would not accept it, nor would banks.

It certainly irked us when we found out that Aberhart's government itself refused to accept scrip in payment for taxes or any other bills. Yet Aberhart's government paid "funny money" for some wages, thereby circulating more scrip and saving itself the expense of using genuine money.

I accepted some scrip as change at the store, but by the time I spent that "funny money," several of the stamps had fallen off the back of the smooth paper, which meant that I had to pay to replace all of the lost stamps or have worthless scrip. I certainly was more reluctant to accept scrip the next time. Every time lost stamps had to be replaced on the back of some scrip, the government made money and the bearer lost money.

Albertans also began to realize that Aberhart should have known he couldn't fulfil any of his election promises. Many of these disillusioned people refused to accept scrip because they no longer trusted anything to do with Aberhart.

Eventually scrip fell into disuse. Within about two years, it had totally disappeared. No one mourned its passing.

Gradually we gave up on our dividends and on the other Social Credit promises. It was a long time, though, before I could tolerate the hymn "Oh, God, Our Help in Ages Past."

LATE FOR SCHOOL

As the depression deepened, Papa became more adamant that there was no money for schooling and that he needed us on the farm. Arnfeld and I were both adults, but Papa's word was still law.

The longer we were out of school, the more desperate we became. Finally we thought of a plan. Arnfeld bravely offered to begin the confrontation. "Papa, Archie and I have an idea, of how we could go to school."

Papa roared, "We have discussed that enough. There is no money."

"But Papa, we'll earn it." Arnfeld spoke quickly then, gathering momentum with each word. "And we'll earn some extra money for the whole family, too. Each summer and fall one of us—Archie or I—could leave the farm and work out for wages while the other stays home and works on the farm without wages."

Papa sat, not saying a word, staring out the window.

Arnfeld swallowed hard and continued. "We'd give some of that money that Archie or I earn, to help support the family. During the winter, either he or I could use the rest of the money to attend school while the other one keeps working here at home."

Papa's arms were still folded in front of his chest.

"We'd each be able to get a year of schooling every two or three years. And we would be able to help the family out."

Papa scowled. "I might think about it."

Under Pastor Nyholm's encouragement, the Dickson High School Association built a girls' dormitory. Esther came up with the idea that she could earn some money working part-time as a cook at the dormitory, and while she was at it she could go to school, too. "No," Papa said.

Esther's grade eight teacher and Pastor Nyholm tried to change Papa's mind. Papa was not pleased. "There is no point in educating girls," he stated. "Girls just get married. Educating them is a complete waste of money."

"Education is never a waste to anyone," said Pastor Nyholm.

"Please let Esther cook at the dorm and go to grade nine at the same time."

"It's a waste to educate anyone who will never use it. And she's needed here to help with the housework and to look after little Paul. Esther's got to learn to work."

So Esther quit school after grade eight. She worked at home for three years until Thora finished grade eight, and then the arguments began again because Thora wanted to work at the dorm and continue school, too.

Finally Papa agreed to let Esther take one more year of school. She worked as a cook at the dormitory and at the same time took both grade nine and ten classes. She passed all of her grade nine and ten final exams that year, but was given official credit for only grade nine because of a government rule allowing only one grade to be "completed" per year.

Thora managed to get to school for grade nine and part of grade ten. Then the depression worsened, and Papa insisted that Thora leave school and work at a full-time job to make money for the family. It didn't seem fair, but Papa refused to budge. "Enough is enough," he said.

Arnfeld and I were luckier. Because of Pastor Nyholm's and our own stubbornness, Papa finally gave in to our plan. For most of the Dirty Thirties, Arnfeld and I took turns going to high school.

The lucky guy who went to school that year would be a month late in starting classes, having had to finish harvest first. Because of the delay in starting the term and with demanding farm chores at home, he'd have trouble keeping up with the lessons.

I sat in my school classes, wondering how to make any sense of what the teacher was saying, trying so hard not to sleep. Each day, all day, at school I fought the exhaustion of early morning rising, late night studying, and the daily grind of heavy farm chores. But somehow it only seemed to make me more determined.

By June 1937, the Great Depression hit rock-bottom, but I had never felt happier. I was almost twenty-seven years old, and had finally finished grade twelve.

My Summer Job

Grain crops were always ripe much earlier in southern Alberta than in our area, so in early August 1937, I hitched rides southward to look for a job.

For many a hot August day, I hitched rides along dusty prairie roads, stopping at each farmyard to beg for work. It seemed that the answer would always be no. How discouraging to be just one of thousands of people in the poverty-stricken prairies searching for work.

Late one evening I looked at a farmyard nestled in a deep coulee. A sparkling creek ran alongside the beautiful old farmhouse. Steep, convoluted banks rose one hundred feet from the valley to flat prairie fields above. It looked idyllic.

But as I headed down the lane into the coulee, I wondered why the farmer had built his ramshackle barn so close to the house when he had lots of room in the coulee.

A few steps farther down the valley, the smell of pigs hit me, nauseating in the sultry air. Then I saw a pig pasture right beside the farmhouse. Why would anybody put his pigs right beside his house?

When I walked into the yard, the pigs squealed as though they were watchdogs. An old man strode from the house, and stood looking up at me like a little soldier, erect, silent, and questioning.

"My name is Archie Morck, and I'm looking for work," I said, trying not to stare at the ragged shirt hanging around his bony neck and chest.

"You've come to the right place. Dollar a day."

"Great!"

"Hope so. Seems hard to keep anybody, even these days." He clenched his jaw. "It'll be regular harvest work. Cutting, binding, and stooking the wheat. In less than a month we should be ready for the threshers." Then he added, "You'll have a few chores every morning before harvesting. Just get the animals in from the field, harness the horses, and milk the cows."

"No problem," I said. "How many cows?"

"Five."

"Sounds good." After all, I had grown up on a farm and worked for plenty of other farmers. A few chores before harvesting seemed a completely reasonable request for an experienced guy like me.

I hardly slept that night. The farmer had given me a bedroom in the attic, baked in summer heat. I opened the window, but choked on the smell of the one hundred or so smelly pigs staring up at me. Never had I seen such skinny pigs. It seemed that this farmer didn't fatten hogs, he thinned them.

The smell from the pig pen made breathing almost impossible. It wasn't much cooler with the window opened anyway, so I closed it, then lay sweltering on my bed, unable to bear even the heat of the worn-out sheet.

I had to have air. Frantically I opened the window again, and climbed back into bed, but the smell of pigs suffocated me. I got up and slammed the window shut.

With the window closed I could barely hear the pigs grunting, but still their smell wafted somehow into that attic, permeating everything. Desperate for air, I opened the window again, then lay tossing and turning, my skin soaked with perspiration.

The frantic squealing of pigs woke me. Gasping for breath I looked out the window. The farmer was pouring slop into the pig trough. Across the valley the beautiful stream shone in the sunshine. I dragged my weary body downstairs and out to the barnyard.

"Good morning," I called.

The farmer nodded. "Noisy little things," he shouted over the squealing.

And smelly, too, I felt like saying, but instead asked as politely as possible, "I, uh, I was wondering why you have your pigs right beside the house?"

"Not so far to carry the slop pail," the farmer replied as he headed toward the barn. "I always keep Charger in the barn at night. That way he's all set for getting the other animals in."

I followed the man into his dusty barn and then out again, as he led a stiff, grey horse blinking into the bright sunlight. The farmer laid his gnarled hand on the old horse's swayed back. This was Charger.

While I saddled Charger, my boss held the halter rope, though it was obvious the ancient horse had no desire to go anywhere.

"You'll find the cows and horses up there," the man said, pointing to the north field high above the valley. "Or maybe they'll be up there," he added, pointing to the *south* field.

"Which field would they most likely be in?" I asked.

"You never know." He shook his head. "Once in a while you might be lucky and find all four horses and all five cows on the first bank you ride up. Sometimes the horses are on one bank and the cows on the other. Sometimes you ride up one bank and they're all on the other side. Like I said, you never know."

I listened, hardly able to believe what I was hearing. "Why don't you build a fence down here to separate the two sides of your pasture?"

"Never time for that kinda thing," the farmer said. "This is just the way we do it. Don't worry, I'll be here with a pail of oats to catch the horses when they go past."

I mounted Charger and prodded the antique steed up the huge, steep bank to the south pasture. By the time we reached the top, the poor old animal was sweating and puffing. The field was empty. I looked north and saw all the horses and cows staring across the valley at me.

It took Charger a good five minutes to climb down the south bank, then twice that long to cross the farmyard and head up the north bank.

Finally we made it to the top and started the chase. The five scrawny cows clambered down the bank to the barnyard. They seemed eager for relief from the pressure of their night's milk production.

The horses, knowing *they* were to be harnessed for a hard day's work, were not quite so eager. My boss stood in the valley, shaking his pailful of oats, ready to entice the horses into the barn where their halters and harnesses were waiting.

Down the bank the horses thundered, totally ignoring the farmer and his oats. Across the valley they raced, splashing through the creek, and galloping up the south bank, while I goaded my stiff mount in pursuit. When Charger managed to crawl up that bank, the chase began all over again.

Around and around the field we went, then finally down the bank, across the valley, through the creek, and up to the north pasture again. This game persisted, up and down the banks. When an exhausted Charger was gasping for breath and barely able to move one leg in front of the other, I stopped him beside the farmer, so frustrated I could hardly keep my voice polite. "Let me build a fence. I'll work on it a little each day."

"No time for that, can't you see?" he said, turning his head from me.

"Then couldn't I keep one of the faster horses in the barn for the morning chase? Why does it have to be Charger?"

"That's the way we do it," said the farmer. "I can't afford hay for any of those young horses when they can be out in the pasture grazing all night."

Off we went again, Charger and I, chasing the horses, while the man stood shaking his pail of oats each time we all thundered by. I don't need a job this badly, I thought. I decided then and there that I'd look for work somewhere else.

Eventually, the horses grew tired and decided to stop; they accepted the oats and followed the farmer into the barn, where he gave them a few wisps of hay. I harnessed the horses while he stood, shoulders back, head high, watching me.

Should I tell him now? But how could I say it? In those days, it was a serious thing to quit a job, a bad reflection on a person's character, something that would make your parents cringe in shame. Besides, this man was paying me so well. A whole dollar a day. I had to have money for college.

"Now, you milk the cows," the man said when I had finished harnessing the horses.

I started to chase the cows towards the barn. "Nope," the farmer said, "I don't use my barn for nothing but harnessing horses." He looked up at me, his face dead serious.

"Why not?"

"Keeps it nice and clean for harnessing horses."

"Where do the cows get milked?"

"In the barnyard."

"What do I tie them to?" This was getting worse and worse.

"Nothing. They'll stand."

"But . . ."

He turned and walked toward the house. "Bring the milk in when you're done. I'll go make us some breakfast."

You don't need to make lunch for me, I thought, because I won't be here. Muttering under my breath, I grabbed the three-legged milk stool and rusty metal pail, then headed for the nearest cow. I perched on the stool, put the pail in the appropriate place, and sure enough, my chosen cow stood quietly while I milked her. Amazing.

There was a major problem, however: the starving razor-back

pigs in the "pasture" right beside the house. Not a blade of grass decorated that so-called pasture. The fence around it was composed of thousands of scraps of board and bits of old rusty wire.

Overwhelmed by the smell of fresh milk, the starving pigs squealed so loudly that my head throbbed from the noise. If I had yelled at the top of my voice, I could not have heard myself.

Just as my pail was half-full, a few of the thinnest pigs managed to escape through gaps in the fence. They raced for my milk pail, pushing and shoving, fighting to plunge their heads into the foaming milk. I tried to fight them off, but they knocked the pail from between my knees, spilling its hard-earned contents all over the ground. And then a pig shoved hard against my legs and tipped the stool out from under me.

I lay in the muddy puddle of spilled milk. The cow moved on. Spitting out a mouthful of mud, I clenched my fists. I was going to get a pail full of milk or die trying.

Leaving the screaming pigs to battle over every drop of dirty milk that my pants hadn't soaked up, I retrieved my pail, and stomped after the cow. When she decided to stop, I set the pail and the stool back in place, and started milking again.

Surely I could get at least that one cow finished before the squealing pigs cleaned up the spilled milk and came at me for more. But other pigs managed to escape from the pen, and mobbed me. Yelling, waving, kicking, I tried to defend the pail. The pigs backed off, glaring at me with round, beady eyes. Then they charged again.

By the time I finally finished milking all five of the cows, those pigs had managed to knock my pail away four more times and they had knocked me on the ground once more. I went in for breakfast exhausted, and completely soaked with milk and mud.

"Ready to get some work done?" asked the farmer.

That does it, I thought. Trembling with anger, I opened my mouth to speak, "I . . . "

"Funny thing," the man said, drawing his scrawny shoulders back as he stabbed at two little pieces of bacon in the frying pan. "So many people can't stick to anything. They just leave." He looked out the window, his eyes focused on something in the distance. "Wife, too. Up and left me, she did. Funny thing."

"I, uh, I'm sorry," I stammered.

He reached for the coffee pot and a loaf of stale-looking bread. "I feel you're different, though, boy. I bet you know how to stick to something."

I sat down, elbows on the dirty tablecloth. I could cover my ears.

I didn't have to listen. I must not let his talking change my mind.

"Yeah," he said, "I can tell you're the kind of guy who isn't scared of a little work."

Don't listen, you don't have to listen, I told myself. Don't let this kind of talk get through to you.

"I bet your parents are proud of having a son who'd never be a quitter," the man added.

I groaned.

"What's wrong?" the farmer asked.

"Oh, nothing." I sighed. I wanted to bury my head in my hands, but instead I told the farmer, "I guess I'd better eat breakfast now so I can get some work done."

Green Suit, Blue Tie

The biggest surprise of all my life came in September 1937. I had just returned home exhausted from harvesting for the crazy farmer in southern Alberta. It had been my turn to work out. The money I earned was supposed to finance my first year of university.

I had worked for several weeks, at least twelve hours a day, but my earnings looked hopelessly inadequate compared to the cost of a year of college. I'd need money not only for tuition but also for room and board. Of course, our anticipated twenty-five-dollar-a-month Social Credit dividend had not materialized, and even I was beginning to admit that it never would. I had just turned twenty-seven, and my chances for more education looked hopeless.

Into our house I walked and sat on the couch, looking around. In the weeks I'd been away nothing had changed. Probably nothing ever would. I'd never get enough money for college, not this year, and not the next nor the next.

My father followed me in and sat down across the room. He cleared his throat. "Archie, um, I've decided to give you $300 to help you go to college."

"Papa!"

"A year at college costs a lot more than $300, I know, but it's absolutely the most that I can afford to give you. You'll have to earn the rest with part-time work." He spoke quickly. "You can leave for Calgary as soon as you want."

"Papa!" was still all that I could manage. And he didn't even say anything about how shameful it was for men to have tears in their eyes.

It turned out that our high school principal, Miss Gundesen, with the help of Pastor Nyholm and now our new Pastor Moller, had finally talked Papa into this.

How Papa had come up with the money I never did find out. Sometimes I wondered if he hadn't been putting away the money that Arnfeld and I had given to the family all those years we'd been taking turns to work out. Or had Mama made some of the $300 by selling her cheeses and other extra farm produce to Uncle Carl's general store?

Miss Gundesen and Pastor Moller thought that Mount Royal College in Calgary would accept late registration. Mount Royal was a small, fully accredited college, operated by the United Church. Tuition, room, and board would cost $450 for one year. I'd need money for books and clothes, too. But somehow I could do it.

Excited and terrified, I took the train to Calgary. In my pocket was Dad's $300 cheque plus my meagre harvest money. I also had sealed letters of recommendation from Miss Gundesen and Pastor Moller, addressed to Dr. Kerby, Principal of Mount Royal College.

But first the matter of clothes. In those days everyone was expected to dress formally for university classes. My farm clothes would hardly be appropriate. I walked the streets of Calgary for hours, looking for the best bargain. Finally I found a green suit with two pair of slacks on sale for twenty-five dollars. I couldn't afford a new necktie, so my old blue tie (the only tie I had ever owned) would have to do, although it certainly didn't match the green.

I put the suit on in the store, and carried my old suitcase to Mount Royal College. It turned out to be a long walk. By the time I arrived it was late afternoon. The registrar looked up when I entered the main office. "Can I help you?" he said in a most unenthusiastic tone, staring at my green suit, then at my old blue tie, then back to the green suit.

I gulped. I could see Dr. Kerby's nameplate on the partially open door to the inner office. "I would like to talk to Dr. Kerby, please."

He raised his eyebrows. "Can you please state your business?"

"I would like to enter Mount Royal College. And I need to ask Dr. Kerby to help me find a part-time job to pay some of my tuition and expenses. I've brought letters of recommendation to Dr. Kerby from my high school principal and my pastor."

He reached out and took the two envelopes. Then, to my horror, he ripped them open and started to read the letters, even though they were clearly addressed to Dr. Kerby.

While the registrar was reading, I was pleading silently, "Please, God, please . . . "

Within seconds the registrar looked up and shook his head. "We definitely cannot accept you. You are several days late for registration. Not only that, you don't have nearly enough money and we can't help you in any way to cover the rest of your expenses. Our janitor jobs are already taken by other students."

He handed me the letters and immediately turned to the work on his desk. I felt sick to my stomach.

Then I heard a voice from Dr. Kerby's office saying, "No, I want to see that young man. Send him in, please."

I walked in, trembling, and stood before a grey-haired, older man with an incredibly kind face. He stood up and grasped my hand firmly. "Please sit down," he said. "We'll see what we can do for you."

I sat in desperate silent prayer while he read my letters of recommendation. Finally he looked up with a gentle smile. "Of course we will take you as a student, Mr. Morck. And we can find you some work to earn the $150 that you still need for tuition, room, and board. When it snows, you can shovel the front sidewalk—it's about half a block long—and you can do some sweeping and clean the blackboards. And when it is really cold you can clean the old coal furnace and carry out the ashes. I don't think you'll find it too hard."

I don't even remember how I thanked him. In fact, I was so overwhelmed that I could hardly find my way out of the room. A miracle had occurred. I was in college!

In the dorm, as I unpacked, my roommate, Del Foote, sat on his bed, trying to get me to chat. I liked his grin. He seemed easygoing, out to enjoy as much as possible of life. Although he was the handsome eighteen-year-old son of a lawyer, and I was a twenty-seven-year-old hayseed, Del could not have been friendlier.

We each had a small closet without doors. Too much aware of the modern clothes lined up in Del's closet, I took off my new green jacket and ancient blue tie to hang in my closet along with my second pair of slacks, two shirts, one sweater, and my old clothes that I'd worn to Calgary. My closet was still almost empty.

At bedtime, Del put on fancy silk pyjamas and a fine bathrobe before he made the trip down the hall to the bathroom.

I was mortified. Never in my life had I money for pyjamas—I'd always slept in my underwear. So I left my trousers on, made the trip down the hall, then took my trousers off and crawled into bed wearing long underwear, prepared for some teasing. Del said nothing.

For a long time I lay awake thanking God for all the wonders the past two days had brought. I was a college student now.

HOW MAMA PAID FOR A PHOTO

The year was 1939. Thora was working in Calgary and had just announced her engagement. Esther had a job in Innisfail, and was busy making marriage plans, too.

Arnfeld and I were both in Calgary at college, planning to finish our last years of university and seminary in the United States. Mama had noticed that her two eldest sons, besides their studies and moving plans, were also showing quite a bit of interest in two young women.

All of these factors made Mama acutely aware of further changes impending in the Morck family.

"Papa," she said, one spring evening, "we should have a professional portrait taken of our family. All eleven of us, while we can still manage to get everybody together."

Papa snorted. "Have you lost your mind? Where would we ever find money for a professional family portrait? We're having a hard enough time with this never-ending depression to find enough money to buy sugar and coffee."

"But this is important. Before they all go off in separate directions. It's probably our last chance. This is our family."

"Important! You'd waste grocery and clothes money for something as frivolous as getting a picture taken. It would probably cost more than Thora or Esther earn in a month. Have you gone crazy?"

"But, Papa."

"Absolutely not. There is no money, no extra money, not for anything. Certainly there's no money for a picture. There is no extra money."

Mama set her chin resolutely. "Then this year I'll raise more chickens."

"More chickens just mean more work looking after them, and more chickens for the coyotes to eat."

Mama couldn't argue with this. No matter how carefully she locked up her chickens in the coop at night, farm chickens did have to roam freely to eat during the day, and a good guard dog was hard to find. In the past couple of summers the coyotes had been very hard on Mama's chicken population.

Still, this was one project that my mother was determined to accomplish. "Well, I'll pray that this summer the coyotes decide that they prefer eating rabbit stew to chicken dinner."

"Who is going to buy all these chickens to eat when you're finished raising them?" Papa asked. "Nobody has any money."

"Well, I'll have to pray about that, too."

Somehow my mother's prayers, which followed her brood of children all through their lifetime, must also have followed her brood of chickens throughout that summer and fall, for it was her most successful year in the poultry business.

Mama didn't buy baby chicks, she always raised her own. She had about twenty hens and a rooster. If any hen started to sit on her nest all day rather than roam the yard, she was called "broody," meaning that the hen would stay to keep fertilized eggs warm for the three weeks that it took to hatch them.

Usually most hens didn't turn broody. They just laid an egg each morning and spent the rest of the day wandering in the yard, eating insects and grass. That year it seemed that a higher than normal number of the hens started to act broody.

Mama had little "brood hen houses" of scrap boards in various places around the yard. She put each broody hen in one of these houses and gave her about a dozen eggs to sit on. Usually some of the eggs didn't hatch. But this year, it seemed as though a high proportion of the eggs did hatch, and soon many hens and their flocks of fluffy yellow chicks were out scratching in the yard in the daytime.

At night Mama carefully locked up each hen and her rapidly growing chicks. The rest of Mama's hens, the non-broody ones, kept producing eggs for our family to eat every day, so that was good, too.

About the beginning of July, Mama noticed that one of her best egg-laying hens had disappeared. Mama assumed the worst, that a coyote had managed to catch her.

Just over three weeks later, Mama came running into the house laughing. "I have a whole extra flock of new chicks!" The missing hen, which had not showed any signs of broodiness, had found a hiding place in the woods, laid her own eggs, and raised a family.

The dozens and dozens of chicks from all of the hens soon lost their fluffiness, started to grow normal feathers, and put on weight with the rich green grass and abundant summer insects, in addition to Mama's grain feedings.

Soon the yard was full of healthy young adult chickens.

That fall, Mama worked very hard, butchering, plucking, and cleaning chickens. The smell of chicken guts and wet feathers hung heavy around the yard each evening when we came home from harvesting, but we thought of all the hungry people that those tender young chickens would feed.

The depression was easing up by then, so Carl Christiansen had no trouble finding buyers in Calgary for Mama's delicious, tender farm chickens. And the prices were surprisingly good.

Mama set a date with George's Photo Studio in Innisfail, twenty-five miles away, which was very far in those days, with horse and wagon and rutty roads.

No one dared to argue. We who had jobs or were in college knew that we had better clear that date on our calendar.

The whole family assembled one afternoon at the studio, preened to look our very best.

The family portrait turned out to be wonderful, a treasure (as Mama had known it would be) to be passed on for generations.

Mama's money from the chickens was enough to order one large picture and nine small ones. The smaller photos were our Christmas gifts from Mama that year. The large photo was framed and placed on our old organ.

That Christmas I smiled as I watched Mama stand in front of the organ, gazing at that family portait with pure joy. "Hey, Mama," I asked, "which are you the most proud of? Us? Or your chickens?"

Mama laughed. And Papa actually managed a good smile.

Other Books by Irene Morck

A Question of Courage
Between Brothers
Tough Trails
Tiger's New Cowboy Boots

Archie Morck was a Lutheran pastor for over thirty years, serving many parishes across Canada (including several country parishes). Archie and his wife, Marion (Hanson), had seven children, of whom Irene is the eldest. Archie Morck died in 1976 at the age of sixty-six. Four of Archie's siblings are still alive at the time of publication of this book: Thora, Alice, Walter, and Ella.